Prepare for the Great Tribulation and the Era of Peace

Prepare for the Great Tribulation and the Era of Peace

Volume IX:
October 1, 1997 – December 31, 1997

by John Leary

Queenship

PUBLISHING COMPANY
P.O Box 42028 Santa Barbara, CA 93140-2028
(800) 647-9882 • (805) 957-4893 • Fax: (805) 957-1631

The publisher recognizes and accepts that the final authority regarding these apparitions and messages rests with the Holy See of Rome, to whose judgement we willingly submit.

– The Publisher

Cover art by Josyp Terelya

©1998 Queenship Publishing

Library of Congress Number # 95-73237

Published by:
Queenship Publishing
P.O. Box 42028
Santa Barbara, CA 93140-2028
(800) 647-9882 • (805) 957-4893 • Fax: (805) 957-1631

Printed in the United States of America

ISBN: 1-57918-066-3

Acknowledgments

It is in a spirit of deep gratitude that I would like to acknowledge first the Holy Trinity: Father, Jesus, and the Holy Spirit, the Blessed Virgin Mary and the many saints and angels who have made this book possible.

My wife, Carol, has been an invaluable partner. Her complete support of faith and prayers has allowed us to work as a team. This was especially true in the many hours of indexing and proofing of the manuscript. All of our family has been a source of care and support.

I am greatly indebted to Josyp Terelya for his very gracious offer to provide the art work for this publication. He has spent three months of work and prayer to provide us with a selection of many original pictures. He wanted very much to enhance the visions and messages with these beautiful and provocative works. You will experience some of them throughout these volumes.

A very special thank you goes to my spiritual director, Fr. Leo J. Klem, C.S.B. No matter what hour I called him, he was always there with his confident wisdom, guidance and discernment. His love, humility, deep faith and trust are a true inspiration.

My appreciation also goes to Father John V. Rosse, my good pastor at Holy Name of Jesus Church. He has been open, loving and supportive from the very beginning.

There are many friends and relatives whose interest, love and prayerful support have been a real gift from God. Our own Wednesday, Monday and First Saturday prayer groups deserve a special thank you for their loyalty and faithfulness.

Finally, I would like to thank Bob and Claire Schaefer of Queenship Publishing for providing the opportunity to bring this message of preparation, love and warnings to you the people of God.

John Leary, Jr.

Dedication

To the Most Holy Trinity

God

The Father, Son and Holy Spirit

The Source of

All

Life, Love and Wisdom

Publisher's Foreword

John has, with some exceptions, been having visions twice a day since they began in July, 1993. The first vision of the day usually takes place during morning Mass, immediately after he receives the Eucharist. If the name of the church is not mentioned, it is a local Rochester, NY, church. When out of town, the church name is included in the text. The second vision occurs in the evening, either at Perpetual Adoration or at the prayer group that is held at Holy Name of Jesus Church.

Various names appear in the text. Most of the time, the names appear only once or twice. Their identity is not important to the message and their reason for being in the text is evident. First names have been used, when requested by the individual.

We are grateful to Josep Terelya for the cover art, as well as for the art throughout the book. Josyp is a well-known visionary and also, the author of *Witness* and most recently *In the Kingdom of the Spirit.*

This volume covers visions from October 1, 1997 through December 31, 1997. The volumes will now be coming out quarterly due to the urgency of the messages. Volume I contains messages from July, 1993 through June, 1994. Volume II contains messages from July, 1994 through June, 1995. Volume III contains messages from July, 1995 through July 10, 1996. Volume IV contains messages from July 11, 1996 through September 30, 1996. Volume V contains messages from October 1, 1996 through December 31, 1996. Volume VI contains messages from January 1, 1997 through March 31, 1997. Volume VII contains messages from April 1, 1997 through June 30, 1997.Volume VIII contains messages from July 1, 1997 through September 30, 1997.

The Publisher

Foreword

It was in July of 1993 that Almighty God, especially through Jesus, His Eternal Word, entered the life of John Leary in a most remarkable way. John is 55 years old and is a retired chemist from Eastman Kodak Co., Rochester, New York. He lives in a modest house in the suburbs of Rochester with Carol, his wife of thirty-two years, and Catherine, his youngest daughter. His other two daughters, Jeanette and Donna, are married and have homes of their own. John has been going to daily Mass since he was seventeen and has been conducting a weekly prayer group in his own home for twenty-five years. For a long time, he has been saying fifteen decades of the Rosary each day.

In April of 1993 he and his wife made a pilgrimage to Our Lady's shrine in Medjugorje, Yugoslavia. While there, he felt a special attraction to Jesus in the Blessed Sacrament. There he became aware that the Lord Jesus was asking him to change his way of life and to make Him his first priority. A month later in his home, Our Lord spoke to him and asked if he would give over his will to Him to bring about a very special mission. Without knowing clearly to what he was consenting, John, strong in faith and trust, agreed to all the Lord would ask.

On July 21, 1993 the Lord gave him an inkling of what would be involved in this new calling. He was returning home from Toronto in Canada where he had listened to a talk of Maria Esperanza (a visionary from Betania, Venezuela) and had visited Josyp Terelya. While in bed, he had a mysterious interior vision of a newspaper headline that spelled "DISASTER." Thus began a series of daily and often twice daily interior visions along with messages, mostly from Jesus. Other messages were from God the Father, the Holy Spirit, the Blessed Virgin Mary, his guardian angel and many of the saints, especially St. Therese of Lisieux. These messages he recorded on his word processor. In the beginning, they were quite short, but they became more extensive as the weeks passed by. At the time of this writing, he is still receiving visions and messages.

These daily spiritual experiences, which occur most often immediately following Communion, consist of a brief vision which becomes the basis of the message that follows. They range widely on a great variety of subjects, but one might group them under the following categories: warnings, teachings and love messages. Occasionally, there are personal confirmations of some special requests that he made to the Lord.

The interior visions contain an amazing number of different pictures, some quite startling, which hardly repeat themselves. In regard to the explicit messages that are inspired by each vision, they contain deep insights into the kind of relationship God wishes to establish with His human creatures. There, also, is an awareness of how much He loves us and yearns for our response. As a great saint once wrote: "Love is repaid only by love." On the other hand, God is not a fool to be treated lightly. In fact, did not Jesus once say something about not casting pearls before the swine? Thus, there are certain warnings addressed to those who shrug God off as if He did not exist or is not important in human life.

Along with such warnings, we become more conscious of the reality of Satan and the forces of evil "...which wander through the world seeking the ruin of souls." We used to recite this at the end of each low Mass. In His love and concern for us, Our Lord keeps constantly pointing out how frail we humans are in the face of such evil angelic powers. God is speaking of the necessity of daily prayer, of personal penance, and of turning away from atheistic and material enticements which are so much a part of our modern environment.

Perhaps the most controversial parts of the messages are those which deal with what we commonly call Apocalyptic. Unusual as these may be, in my judgment, they are not basically any different than what we find in the last book of the New Testament or in some of the writings of St. Paul. After a careful and prayerful reading of the hundreds of pages in this book, I have not found anything contrary to the authentic teaching authority of the Roman Catholic Church.

The 16th Century Spanish mystic, St. John of the Cross, gives us sound guidelines for discerning the authenticity of this sort of phenomena involving visions, locutions, etc. According to him, there are three possible sources: the devil, some kind of self-imposed hypnosis or God. I have been John's spiritual confidant for over three years. I have tested him in various spiritual ways and I am most confident that all he has put into these messages is neither of the devil nor of some kind of mental illness. Rather, they are from the God who, in His love for us, wishes to reveal His own Divine mind and heart. He has used John for this. I know that John is quite ready to abide by any decision of proper ecclesiastical authority on what he has written in this book.

Rev. Leo J. Klem, C.S.B.
Rochester, New York
1993

Visions and Messages
of John Leary:

Wednesday, October 1, 1997: (St. Therese's Feast)

After Communion, I could see a bright gleaming stairway going up to Heaven. St. Therese stood there and said: *"My friends, you know how much of a fighter I am to save souls. All of you need to have this same fervor. This stairway is the goal to lead all souls up this path to Jesus. Do not shirk your duty to save souls, but go forward and do not waste your time on unproductive things. Those things done to help God in saving your neighbor are the most important and should deserve top priority in your list of duties. Do not be lackadaisical in your efforts, but become rooted in faith to be a fighter for Christ — a prayer warrior to fight evil. Once you see the fruit of this mission of saving souls, it should encourage you more to step up your efforts. How many times has the Lord told you that time is short? So, go forward doing whatever you can do personally to bring more souls to Jesus."*

Thursday, October 2, 1997: (Guardian Angels' Feast)

After Communion, I could see a guardian angel protecting someone from the demons. Mark, my angel, came and said: *"I stand before God and I submit to His permission to speak to you. It is right that I respond to our comparison to tooth fairies as irresponsible. I know this is strong language for you, but our duty to care for you is not a laughing matter. Also, to suggest even for a second that we do not exist, is challenging the Scriptures and God's love in sending us. Our help is very evident in people's lives whether they wish to acknowledge it or not. We will have an even more important role in helping you through the tribulation. You have told the people of our power which will be shown you even more in time to come. Never doubt the Lord's protection through our presence. I am giving you assurance that God's power is almighty and evil temptations are only allowed as a test. We are the ones urging your good behavior, so remember our thoughts first over any evil inclinations."*

Later, at the prayer group, I could see several popes and then John Paul II. He was suffering in pain. Jesus said: *"My people, pray for the poor Holy Father, because he suffers much for My Church. There is mounting opposition to his papacy as evil is preparing to overthrow him. Much like I had to suffer at the hands of My people, he also will be persecuted for My Name's sake. He needs your prayers both for his health and the strength to keep the schismatic church at bay."*

I could see some pictures of angels and statues in a back room representing how they have been taken out of the churches. Jesus said: *"My people, some older churches still have statues and icons of the saints and angels. Many of these heavenly remembrances have been removed in the supposed renovation of your many altars. Many churches have been stripped clean of the angels and only unreal modern sculptures are present. Why have you allowed others to take away your heritage in remembering the communion of saints and the angels as well? On this feast day of your guardian angels which I have assigned to each of you, give thanks to God for your guardians."*

I could see St. Therese and Mother Teresa. St. Therese said: *"My dear souls, look how much people all over the world have honored Mother Teresa, one of my namesakes. By doing your little way in living to help others, you will be accomplishing many good works of mercy. Even a little service to you means a great deal to those in Heaven. All Heaven is watching your actions. Be a good representative for God's faithful by doing all that you can to help the poor little ones who have no one to care for them."*

I could see a baseball stadium and St. Therese came again and said: *"My little one, please take note to put your time to better use in not watching the TV sports. If you have so much time, you should put it to a better use for God. Remember that you have to account to God for all that you do. Do not disappoint Jesus in wasting any time at your disposal. Much prayer and help for sinners are in much need at this time."*

I could see a young girl and she passed through various ages to a young lady. Jesus said: *"My people, you need to act as spiritual guardians for the souls of your children. Train them in good prayer habits and witness your prayer petitions to show them how God can help them. Pray at meals, at bedtime and any other time that you can say the Rosary together. By your example, you can watch how your influence will guide your children on their path to Heaven. If your children should wander away, help them gently back to My fold. Never let them out of your spiritual sight."*

I could see some young children being taught in school. Jesus said: *"My parents, it is your responsibility to see what your children are being taught. No matter what grade they are in, even college, ask them what is being taught. They could be getting evil influences that you would not know about. Sometimes your concern for their souls may alert them to the evil things going on in the schools. Teach them as well spiritually, as they receive education about worldly things. Your care must be constant and gently persistent in order to keep them from bad influences."*

I could see a long red stairway which led up to Heaven. Jesus said: *"My people, when you look toward Heaven, it seems so distant and hard to imagine your coming to Heaven. Consider each day of your life as one step closer along this stairway. Each day has its trials and you may find it difficult at times to carry on. When life is troubling, place your burdens on My shoulder and I will help you on your way. Never give up, but keep struggling, for your goal of endless life with Me is most consoling. You may suffer hard times, but My grace will ease your troubles, so you may take an occasional spiritual rest. Seek Me in retreats when you need to be strengthened. A spiritual vacation may be more needed than your worldly vacations."*

Friday, October 3, 1997:

After Communion, I could see some high seas with a foaming wave. Jesus said: *"My people, these churning seas are like the unsettled waters in your society today. Many souls are wandering with no direction except their own fancy. There will be coming some serious events which will upset many from their comfortable lifestyle. You people of America are like the cities con-*

demned in the readings, today. You are taken up so much with yourselves that you fail to see the decay in your morals. If you do not come to your senses and convert your lives from sin, these cleansing waves may destroy your complacency and apathy. I am looking for My souls to have some body and fight for the moral high ground and not be complacent with inactivity. If you do not fight upstream to assert your faith, you will be washed downstream into the abyss of the pit in Hell."

Later, at Adoration, I could see a man wearing a Western black hat and behind him was a ghost town of boarded up old buildings. Jesus said: *"My people, you have seen many ghost towns out west from the gold rush days. I tell you, you will see more towns coming under such pressure as your industries in these towns start to fail. When the main employers vacate their factories, the people will leave with them. Just as these cities in My day brought condemnation upon themselves, so you will be seeing similar happenings in your evil age. When men fail to focus their lives on Me, you will see them go down to bitter ruin depending only on themselves."*

Saturday, October 4, 1997: (St. Francis of Assisi)

After Communion, I could see a grandfather clock turned upside down. Jesus said: *"My people, I am turning your world upside down when I come. The proud and famous people, who were first, will be last. The poor and destitute will be first to enter into Heaven. That is why I have told you that you must come to Me in faith as little children, never filled with pride, but accepting Me as Lord of your life. Again, I come soon to remove evil from this world. The devil and evil people will be chained in Hell. The earth I will renew and remove all of man's destruction of My creation. After the defeat of the Antichrist, man will again experience paradise as I will make everything new. My faithful will rejoice, while the wicked will mourn the end of their sinful enjoyment. Life, as you know it, will be changed dramatically, back to the way I intended without the influence of evil."*

Later, after Communion, I could see a long corridor with many people on either side. There was a sense of time as you went down the aisle that all of humanity had its roots in Adam. Jesus said: *"My people, I am showing you about your origins from the first man. Many of your theologians have taken liberties in their interpretation of Genesis. I have told you before that the creation account is the belief that I have revealed to you. This vision of humanity descending from one man is true and it is not meant to be debated. Do not be concerned with the gender of terms when you read these accounts. I have made you male and female and every soul is equal before Me. It is the people telling you that these accounts are myths, that should concern you. The biblical writers I inspired with the Holy Spirit were to give you My revelation in terms that you could understand. All that was described has come to pass and all that is foretold will come to pass. You need to discern with the grace of the Holy Spirit whenever someone gives you their interpretation of the scriptures. Listen to the writings of the Church Fathers when there is any question of interpretation. My Church is your guardian of the Faith. Listen to My Magisterium for the truth on these subjects."*

At Adoration, I could see a monstrance with a bright light all around it. There was a great tingling of spiritual energy which came over me. Jesus said: *"My people, when you come before My Blessed Sacrament, you receive special graces for your adoring Me. When you fix your gaze on Me, you are graced to see My Real Presence before you. Your all powerful God is before you where I have condescended Myself to be a prisoner for you under the appearance of bread. I am here for you in this form, because you could not humanly stand before My glory, unless I granted a grace for this. The power that you felt in your body is the radiance of My true glory that flows from My Host. Be thankful for any opportunity to visit My Blessed Sacrament and My reception in Holy Communion. Remember to be free from mortal sin to receive My Eucharist for fear of committing a sin of sacrilege. I invite all of My faithful to come to Me at any time so I can strengthen your faith and enhance your belief in the mystery of My Real Presence. Go forward from your visit and carry Me into all you do in life. Take Me with you wherever you go and witness My love to all of mankind."*

Sunday, October 5, 1997:

At Deacon Sam Salamone's chapel of the Blessed Sacrament, I could see a staircase around a pillar like we saw at Zaragosa, Spain at Our Lady of the Pillar. Our Lady gave the message: *"My dear children, I came as a pillar of faith to strengthen St. James. He needed this stamina of my help in his missionary work. This is the same pillar of faith that I need to be for the faithful at this time. Many have been overwhelmed with a flood of evil that has them drifting further away from their roots in my Son, Jesus. I am that pillar of prayer that you can grab onto to hold fast in your faith. By using my weapon of the Rosary in prayer, you can overcome any evil force that you may encounter. My children, listen to my call to stay close to your roots in Jesus. It is by His grace that you will win your salvation. That is why I always lead you to my Son, since He is the only one that your soul can ever have rest in. Heed His call, for your time of judgment has arrived."*

Monday, October 6, 1997:

At Adoration, I could see some gambling tables and people losing their money. Jesus said: *"My son, do not worry if you should be persecuted for My Name's sake. You may experience harassments from the evil one every time that you proclaim My Word and seek conversion for sinners. You may even lose things or have them stolen. Even if you should be stripped of all you have, do not worry, since I will be helping you at your side. Many of My prophets had to suffer insults, beatings, and even some, martyrdom. When you give Me your all, do not hold anything back, but go forward preaching My Word, no matter what may befall you. Stay close to Me in prayer and do not count on everything being rosy. There will be sufferings, but your joy will be in seeing many souls saved in conversion. So speak out when you have the opportunity to witness to My Word. Continue this mission right up to your dying day. My love envelops all those doing My Will. Those who follow My commands will receive a glorious reward with Me."*

Tuesday, October 7, 1997: (Feast of Our Lady of the Rosary)

After Communion, I could see people present at daily Mass. Mary came and said: *"My dear children, blessed are you who come*

*in humble submission each day to do your duty in following my
Son, Jesus. While some would claim to follow their own pursuits,
it is being in obedience to the Divine Will that each of you are
called. Souls were not placed here to do everything on their own,
but as creatures of God you are called to be in His service. My
Son, Jesus, calls you to love God and your neighbor in all that
you do. When you see how you fit into God's plan, you can see
why it is more important to follow His Will than your own will.
The world teaches independence and doing things on your own,
but each of you are called to a higher order of God's command.
Do not think in following God that the majority should rule only
by itself. When God created you, you were asked freely to love
Him and obediently to submit to His Will. It is the pride of ruling
over your own life that you must struggle with every day. By living
for God in your spiritual and earthly life, you will find your salvation. Think only of what God wants for you and that will be enough
for you. You have seen in my life how I directed all of my actions
to pleasing God. This is my example for you to do the same."*

Later, at Adoration, I could see soldiers digging some mass
graves. Jesus said: *"My people, I have told you in the past, when
you saw the mass graves of people killed in Bosnia, that this would
happen here. Man will be so influenced by the Antichrist that his
agents will seek out the believers to kill them. Once they have
martyred these people, they will also dispose of their bodies by
crematoriums or mass graves. This extent of persecution you have
not known in America. This is why I am preparing My people
spiritually and physically to be able to endure this trial. With faith
in Me, I will protect your souls from the demons. Those who are
martyred will rise again to enjoy My Era of Peace. Have no fear,
My people, this pain will be over quickly as a mother gives birth
to her child. Her pain is quickly forgotten for the joy of bringing
a new life into the world. So it is with the tribulation. Once you
witness the Era of Peace, your joy will quickly forget your pain-
ful moments. Have hope, My people, since ridding this evil from
the earth will be coming soon. I love all of you so much and I ask
you to pray much for your strength in this time to stand up to
your persecutors. Love everyone and you will have riches stored
up in Heaven for you."*

Wednesday, October 8, 1997:

After Communion, I could see some trees in the sun on the ground, and as I looked higher, there was the majesty of some mountains. Jesus said: *"My people, look to yourselves to correct your faults and do not make judgments on others. It is easy for you to notice faults in others, but you do not want to acknowledge your own faults. If you are seeking perfection in My love, you must look on a higher plane in following My judgments than your own. As you look at everyone including yourselves, you can see why I am so merciful. You have weakness to sin because of the effects of Original Sin. You must turn your pride aside and accept that all of you are sinners. Then you must seek My forgiveness to keep your souls clean by the Sacrament of Reconciliation. Work on your own faults and you will have plenty to correct, before criticizing others for the same faults. Look to be an example of a good life to others rather than seeking judgment of others."*

Thursday, October 9, 1997:

After Communion, I could see a football brass trophy. Jesus said: *"My people, do not follow the ways of a worldly man who performs all of his actions to gain praise from others. For these souls, they are driven by gain for money to be important or by their skills to be famous among men. My children, it is more important that you perform your deeds to please Me. When you perform deeds out of love for Me and your neighbor, you are honoring Me. When you do these deeds, not to gain money or fame, you are storing up treasure in Heaven. You see then a drawing to please Me out of love. All of these acts of love are more fulfilling than all the money you could ever receive. When I repay you for even your secret good deeds, your graces are worth more than if you were a king or a president. All of this life's activities come down to how you love Me and your neighbor. All other reasons are done out of selfishness. When you strive to imitate My life, you will see loving Me gives you an inner joy and peace which the world can never provide."*

Later, at the prayer group, I could see a bright moon. Then I saw an eclipse of the sun by the moon. Mary came and said: *"My dear children, you need to be praying fervently, that there will be no problem with the nuclear powered satellite. I am showing you the moon because I am like the lesser light compared to my Son, Jesus. This time of the eclipse will signal some great events which are to take place. Be prepared for the coming tribulation."*

I could see a table with some old love letters laid out in a bright light. Jesus said: *"My people, there are some souls who loved Me very much in years gone by, but now the distractions of the world have taken them from Me. Keep your love for Me burning each day as the fervor of your first encounter. You need to be struggling to do better in your spiritual life. If you forget Me in prayer just one day, you could endanger your soul, as many interests seek your attention. You must remember your prayers every day or you could be snatched away from Me. Seek also to bring back these old lovers of mine. They need your help at this time."*

I could see a night scene representing this evil age being turned like a page in history. It opened up to a new bright world of beautiful harmony among plants and animals. Jesus said: *"My people, you are blessed to be living in this age which is about to be renewed as an extension of the creation of a new era. You will see the evil ones chained in Hell at last, as My justice and love will reign over the earth. The Antichrist's brief reign will come to a quick end and the hope for My peace will be realized. Give thanks to God that you have been blessed to be a part of My faithful remnant."*

I could see some troops in the Mid-East looking out of a watch tower. Jesus said: *"My people, I have urged you to pray for peace in the world, especially among the Arab lands. There are rumors of war in this area, and it is on the verge of open hostilities. If war does come to this area, many nations may become involved and your oil supplies will be threatened. Seek to support the peace overtures or unheard of war may ensue."*

I could see a large, dark, secret building open and there were large laser weapons poised for testing. Jesus said: *"My dear people, why do you seek to make more dangerous weapons and test things which could cause great harm to the earth? It is time to stop this weapons research before there may be some catastrophic accidents. Voice your opinion and your prayers for this activity to cease. The Antichrist will use all of these weapons against you."*

I could see many bodies in caskets being paraded, and some men cast some blank stares at this scene. Jesus said: *"My people, if you could see every aborted baby paraded down your streets in a casket, you would be appalled. It is because these bodies are burned and buried in dumps that you are not aware of this grisly business right under your nose. Think of the millions of these reported deaths and realize that it is happening in your very hospitals. If this shedding of blood is not stopped, your future will see My justice. Fight against abortions in any way that you can speak out. If you do not act and pray to stop abortions, you will be unconsciously condoning it."*

I could see a basement where some extra food was being stored. Jesus said: *"My son, you have seen many critics of the food that I asked each of you to store. People criticized Noah for building his Ark and Joseph for saving seven years of food. But because I directed this activity, these scoffers lived to regret their criticism. The evil people will use food as a means to control people through the Mark of the Beast. I will provide for your needs, but I will employ your food stocks to help the faithful in their hunger. You will need this before the tribulation. As the Antichrist declares himself, I will provide your food wherever you are through My manna. Have faith and hope in My Words to feed you in your need. I will not abandon you in this trial."*

Friday, October 10, 1997:

After Communion, I could see a large, blue-green sea. Jesus said: *"My people, for those who have not understood that you are in the end days, the storms about to occur will hold your attention. Many think there is nothing changing, but these people may regret this statement. Your time of mercy has expired and your day of judgment will test you as you have never been tested before. As you are coming close to the time of tribulation of the Antichrist, prepare yourself for a battle of good and evil that will show you a test of powers. Your spiritual stamina will be tested and you must seek My help in this time or you will surely be lost. I am sending My angels to help in this battle with the demons. Seek their help, since the evil of your day will soon reach its peak. In the twinkling of an eye, I will then bring all evil to sudden destruction. I will bring you an Era of Peace which all of My faithful are seeking."*

Later, at Adoration, I could see a monstrance from behind and there were three pieces of manna in the monstrance. Jesus said: *"My people, when you see My Blessed Sacrament, you are seeing Three Persons in One God. Where I am, the Father and the Holy Spirit are there also. I thank all of those faithful who come to visit Me in adoration. For those who reach out to Me, I am there in their midst bestowing My graces upon you. Always remember to come and visit Me. You all have been given many gifts, but few come back to thank Me. Work hard every day, My people, to gain in your faith. You need to be always moving forward in your spiritual life without looking back. My graces are here for the asking. Do not be bashful in coming forth to receive what I offer you. You are the one who must make the forward move to accept Me into your life. Go and walk with Me by your side and all Heaven will greet you when you come home to Me."*

Saturday, October 11, 1997:

After Communion, I could see Mary before a small audience and she called me over to talk to them. Mary said: *"My son, I am calling you forward to go and preach the words of my Son, Jesus. Listen to the words of Scripture that He is calling on you today to follow His Call and His Will. You have been blessed with many messages, and it is your duty to share them with my faithful remnant. This group you are meeting today are very devoted to me and my Son, Jesus. Welcome them today with my greetings and encourage them in prayer as I have asked all of my children to pray. Continue to pray for my intentions of poor sinners, the souls in Purgatory that I visit, and especially the lost souls who need your intercession. Many souls are languishing in their sins and they need someone to show them the way to my Son. I encourage all of my faithful to listen to my Son, Jesus' words to go and evangelize those around you, who may be lost without your help. Now more than ever is the time to seek conversions, for these souls are on the brink of Hell, unless they return to my Son, Jesus."*

Later, at Leticia Villar's house in Bedminster, N.J., after Communion, I could see a scene outside among nature. There was again a vision of the beautiful trees turning colors. Jesus said: *"My people, as you view My animals in the field and My little creatures all around you, you have a small sense of the beauty of My creation. Again, as you are witnessing the show of colors in the trees, you can appreciate how extensive and intricate are the workings of My creation. None of this can happen by chance, that is why everything receives a gift of its existence from Me. I have created all of mankind and I find you and everything that I have created very good. You have been made less than perfect because of the effects of Original Sin. I have promised to redeem you and all of you will be resurrected one day into My glory, for those who are faithful. Be thankful for all of creation and especially for the life that you are experiencing. But please, My children, do not violate your life or the lives of another, even the unborn. You would not have wanted your life terminated before you were born, so do not take any one else's life either. See that I have a plan for all of you to follow and it is your duty to give Me your will so I can accept you into your eternal home in Heaven. I ask you to have your sins forgiven in Confession and stay close to Me until your death. I will reward your faithfulness with a loving peace forever with Me."*

Sunday, October 12, 1997:

At Leticia Villar's house in Bedminster, N.J., after Communion, I could see a bright light on the bloom of a beautiful flower arrayed in beautiful colors. Jesus said: *"My people, I have asked you to bloom where you are planted. You look at the lilies of the field and they do not keep their gift of beauty to themselves, they share it with the whole world. So it is with you, I have called you in love to share your love with Me and your neighbor. Do not keep your beauty secret, but go and share your gift of faith with everyone. Do not be selective in your sharing, but shine forth your love on your friends and those that you dislike as well. Imitate your Lord. My light and love shines on the good and the bad. So, follow My example and love all of mankind and you will win over even those souls far from Me. See that your love is unconditional as Mine, for each soul is lovable as I created you to love Me."*

Monday, October 13, 1997:

After Communion, I could see an altar with a large glass chalice. Jesus said: *"My people, many want to drink the cup of pleasure from the world, instead of My cup of suffering. You would rather follow your own choices, than be in obedience to My Will. So it is that some are saying the Mass with their own ideas in place of what My Church teaches. Man is violating My spiritual laws as well as My physical laws against nature. Do you think that all of these abominations will go unanswered? I tell you, for those who test Me, their cup of wrath is overflowing and they will soon taste of My justice. I have offered you many opportunities in My mercy, but you have taken advantage of My kind heart to grow worse in your sins. You will soon see the consequences of your actions culminate in My stripping of your gifts. How can I continue to bless you with My gifts, if you are not listening to My commands? When you fall in ruin, you will understand how you have been violating My Will."*

Later, at Adoration, I could see a bishop and many faithful being shot down in a massive slaying. Jesus said: *"My people, there are many evil factions that wish to kill My clergy. You have seen such instances in your news reports, and they will become more frequent as My enemies grow in strength. Be aware, My faithful, that your lives will be endangered as persecution of My Church becomes more open. Not only will you be persecuted from without, but even within My Church, masonic elements will be creating a schism. You will find it difficult to have places of worship for those that follow My pope son. When you see these things taking place, you will know that you are in the apostasy before the Antichrist's coming. I love you, My people, and I will do everything to help you through this evil era. Come, follow Me and I will see to your spiritual protection. Be thankful that soon all of this evil will be vanquished. Know, My followers, that I am in full control, and I am only permitting this evil as a test of your faith. Remain close to Me, no matter how severely you will be tested."*

Tuesday, October 14, 1997:

After Communion, I could see some rockets going and coming in dark space. Jesus said: *"My people, man has taken some considerable risks in his curiosity to discover about other planets. Your current endeavor (Casini Space Probe) is another example of technology at risk. People have trusted your understanding of science to expect success most of the time. What is not fully appreciated are the dangers in spreading this toxic plutonium all over the earth. Even if the odds of success are appealing, any chance of failure should be well planned out. Pray, again, that man in his quest for knowledge does not consume himself. This curiosity has plenty of opportunity to kill thousands of people. If you continue to expose yourselves to such dangers, you may reap the whirlwind of any accidents. Encourage your scientists not to be taking such liberties with people's lives. Civilizations before you have destroyed themselves in just such abandonment of reason and safety."*

Later, at Adoration, I could see a large crocodile with its mouth open and showing its teeth. Jesus said: *"My people, I will not allow the jaws of death to influence you until you have made your peace with God. My mother's mantle and scapular will come to your aid before your death. The Gates of Hell also will not prevail against My Church. I am watching over all of your souls, and I am looking out to keep the devil from distracting and stealing souls from Me. You must be spiritually prepared and ready to die at any time. If you are the servant found watching for Me, I will welcome you into My banquet. If you are making merry with this world's things and you are called home, then you will be like the thief who will be tied and thrown into the night to wail and grind his teeth. So My lesson to you is to always be prepared, for you know not the hour of My coming for you."*

Wednesday, October 15, 1997:

After Communion, I could see a 5-pointed star imbedded in metal about an inch deep. Then I saw this shape extend out by itself making an elongated star shape in metal. Jesus said: *"My people, do not be taken in by demonic symbols such as pentagrams, crystals or any other of these New Age charms or hexes. All of these things that invoke evil spirits are to be avoided, even if they look innocent and unprovoking. So it is also with literature on the Antichrist or his teachings. All of these things should be cast out of your house to remove any possible influence on you. As the tribulation draws nearer, evil forces will gain in power. On the other hand, it is important to keep your blessed sacramentals on your person. Carry a Cross with My Corpus, your Rosary and your scapular. You will need protections from the evil ones and no means by which these demons can influence you. By calling on My Name and seeking My protection, you will be safeguarded even in this evil age."*

Thursday, October 16, 1997: (St. Margaret Mary-Sacred Heart) After Communion, I could see an altar and then a curved narrow smooth cave. Jesus said: *"My people, My love is poured out for you as a libation. I gave My life for all of mankind on the Cross in testimony to My love for you. How much more can your God love you, if I shed My blood for your salvation? Even in these end days My love will be with My faithful in a miraculous way, guiding you to places of safety. I will provide shelter for you in the caves that you should be grateful. You should know that I love each soul, and I do everything to afford each soul an opportunity to reach Heaven. For those that do not make it to Heaven, they have chosen for themselves to reject Me and embrace the world. This devotion to My Sacred Heart is your attempt to know and appreciate My love for you as you return your love to Me. Show Me how much you love Me each day by telling Me in your words, prayers and actions. When you truly are reaching out to Me from your heart, you will see how our two hearts are joined in love."*

Later, at the prayer group, I could see some jets going off into the dark and there were some explosions. Jesus said: *"My people, I am showing you the start of a war to come. Many nations may become involved. Again, I ask you to pray much for peace in the world. If you allow the evil one to control your pride, many will be willing to fight to the death. The nations in the Mid-East will continue to build hostilities toward one another. If you cannot have peace among yourselves, how can you have peace among nations?"*

I could see some stars and distant planets. Jesus said: *"My people, you continue to seek knowledge of the origins of the universe. Again, your curiosity of other worlds has driven your search* to immense proportions. Do not be curious of things that you cannot change. Also, focus your energies on Me for any revelation necessary to reach Heaven. If you sought Heaven with the same energy that you seek things of the world, surely there would be less souls going to Hell."

I could see a rose on a memorial of someone who was killed. Jesus said: "My people, your media is making many atrocities available for your viewing. The brutality and senseless killing going on is an indication of how evil your generation has become. Unless your world turns to Me for help in your sins, you will see even more killings. Come to your senses, My people, or your society may soon be wiped out with its madness."

I could see a blue sky and a very dark mountain. Jesus said: "My people of America, I am showing you the calm before the storm. Plans are being made for United Nations troops to control your people in the detention centers. Many do not want to believe that this can happen, but these troops and foreign tanks already are in place for your occupation. Look at the military activity on your roads and in your forests and you will see their preparations. Pray to Me and your angels for helping you against these evil forces."

I could see Mary coming in the clouds as she looked over her children. Mary said: "Listen, my children, to my daughter in Conyers. These messages on a coming war are why I am constantly asking for your prayers for peace in the world. Turn your hearts toward God or these flames of war will consume you. Work at saving souls and bringing them to my Son while you can still move about freely. There will come a time when the messages will cease and you will have to deal with the Antichrist and his agents. This is the time when you will have to trust and hope in my protection and that of my Son."

I could see a woman in the kitchen preparing some food to store away. Jesus said: "My people, you must be like the wise virgins who went out to get oil for their lamps for the wedding. Do not be like the five foolish virgins who made no preparation at all. When I tell you to store food now, it is from My mercy that I am preparing you. I will help those even in the eleventh hour, but unless you trust in My help, you will surely be lost."

I could see a beautiful cross on a grave in the cemetery. Jesus said: *"My people, as the readings on the judgment and the end times come upon you, you need to give serious thought about the state of your soul. These readings speak of being forever vigilant when I will return for your soul. Seek My forgiveness in frequent Confession, and you will have nothing to fear. It is those who are in serious sin that should fear for their lives. It is your spiritual life that is most important. Those without grace will be cast into the eternal fires. Seek to be close to Me and encourage the lost souls back to Me in whatever way you can get them to come. This is a call to all souls that you need to be ready now more than ever. When the evil one assumes power, you will be swallowed up in his grasp if you do not have Me in your heart."*

Friday, October 17, 1997:

After Communion, I could see the sole of a big shoe come pressing down on me. Jesus said: *"My people, you need to be observant of how the one world people will be oppressing you financially and spiritually. Your jobs are gradually being changed to lesser paying jobs. Your benefits are being removed all for the sake of the rulers of money to keep you subservient to your employers. The same is occurring with your churches. Through the threat of finances, many Church men are afraid to speak out against sin or any of the real issues of your life such as abortion, sins of the flesh, killing and theft in various forms. My people, these rulers over you want to keep you poor and under their control. They are afraid even if you want to follow Me in your religion. Soon you will be persecuted for your beliefs and they will attack you through your jobs as well. Pray to Me for strength in these hard times, for soon I will conquer all of these evil men. Endure this trial for a short time and all of your needs will be cared for beyond your dreams. Strive for a spiritual wealth of My graces and do not be so concerned with the elusive wealth in the world which will rot tomorrow."*

Later, at Adoration, I could see Our Lady handing out Rosaries to the people and one was a nun dressed in white robes. Mary said: *"See, my children, how I bring you my Rosaries and I encourage you to pray. As you see me descending, I am asking all of my devotees to pray as I meet each of you at different levels of spirituality. Even the saints found time to pray my Rosary. I am an obedient servant of my Son and I seek many souls to be joined with my Son in prayer. See that my Jesus calls out to all sinners to come to Him for help. Jesus and I never give up on any soul to be saved. Many have tried to hide themselves from Jesus so they could keep from committing their lives to Him. Too many souls want to follow their own consciences rather than submit to my Son's Will. No matter how much some would rather refuse their responsibility of being in obedience to God and their superiors, they still are being sought by my Son. Do not give up on these souls as we do not, and strive to help all souls searching for a lasting peace. This can only be found in God, and my faithful need to convey that message to these lost souls. Pray for the grace to evangelize and witness to all those you come in contact with."*

Note: Due to travel and the late talk, there were no opportunities for messages on Saturday.

Sunday, October 19, 1997:

At All Souls Church, San Francisco, California, after Communion, I could see a large cross with a bright light opening up on it. I then saw someone wearing a cross around their neck. Jesus said: *"My people, in the Gospel I asked My Apostles if they could drink from the same cup of pain as I had to endure. Now, I am asking My faithful if you are ready to take up your cross of suffering each day. See, My friends, that your life is a struggle and not very easy at times. You must be willing to offer up to Me all of your hurts and disappointments. When you are feeling down, call on Me and I will help you in carrying your cross. Do not give up or despair in your problems, but look on them as a means to build your faith in Me. You do not need much to live on in this world, so do not be striving for riches and be sad when money problems test you. You need to lift up your spirits and be happy to live each day in My service. Again, be proud that you are a follower of Mine and show that love by wearing My Crucifix. This will be a witness to others of your belief and show that you are not afraid of criticism to display it. Many times I have told you, that unless you publicly witness to Me before men, I will not speak of you to My Father. So go forward and witness My love even in environments that may be difficult for you to publicly display your beliefs.*"

Later, after a spiritual Communion, in San Francisco, California, St. Therese was seen as a Carmelite nun in a brown habit. She said: *"My dear children, this is an honor on my one hundredth anniversary to be made a Doctor of the Church. This is an example to all of you that a simple, fervent life can be offered up to Jesus and receive many merits. Being a saint is not a complicated thing, it involves a spiritual persistence to seek perfection through suffering and a humble life. There are many things that you are asked to suffer, and the hardest is to surrender your will to God. The more of your Purgatory that you suffer on earth, the more is your chance of going straight to Heaven as a saint of God. So set your sight on gaining your crown of salvation through faithful service to Jesus and He will not turn aside your request. Keep your heart one with His and keep your souls forever pure before Him. The Lord loves you for all of your efforts to perfect yourself for Him."*

Monday, October 20, 1997:

After Communion, I could see some angels come and then a warrior came on a white horse. Jesus said: *"My people, time is short as I am showing you Myself coming as the first of the Four Horsemen. I am bringing My angels to help you in this last battle against evil. I am preparing you for all of the seals that the angels are about to unleash against the earth. Evil has been permitted its time and now you will soon see the demons and the angels clash in a final battle. Do not be afraid at this time to go out and fight the evil ones, for I will strengthen you and My faithful to win this battle for Me. The angels will be your guides and the Antichrist and his lot will be defeated. Rejoice, My people, for evil will be chained in Hell in utter defeat. This is My prophecy and as you see these events unfold, you will find them marvelous to behold. Just as I wielded My power against the forces of the Egyptian army in the Exodus, you will see My hand again gain a glorious victory against Satan and all his demons. Be joyful that this time is upon you."*

Later, I could see some people and there were fumes about them as you would see a mirage over a hot surface. Jesus said: *"My people, do not allow the evil one and the false prophets to lead you into confusion. I am Truth and My Words are true. All that was prophesied of Me, has come to be. All that is foretold in the Scriptures, will come to be as well. Look to My Church and the Magisterium led by my pope son, John Paul II for guidance in understanding My Words. My Commandments are unchangeable and the traditions of My Church are to lead you. There will come a time and you are seeing it now, where theologians and priests will twist the meaning of My Words. Pray for the discernment of My Holy Spirit to know the truth. You will see the false witness come as an imposter pope who will try to mislead you in errors. Do not follow this man of iniquity who will lead souls in error to follow the Antichrist in blasphemy. Trust the teachings of Pope John Paul II and you will be saved. This confusion will spread among you, but its source will be from the evil one."*

Tuesday, October 21, 1997:

After Communion, I could look down on a table as a sacrificial altar. Jesus said: *"My people, in the readings, today, you are seeing one man's sacrifice of My life that has brought you salvation from one man's sin by Adam. Those of you who attend daily Mass are even more attuned to this reality of My suffering for you. The Mass itself is an unbloody sacrifice of My Body and Blood which is a remembrance of My death for you. You hear these same words repeated at each Mass so you can know My all encompassing love for mankind through which I have freed you from your Original Sin. I have earned Heaven for you, but you must seek to have your actual sins forgiven through My Sacrament of Reconciliation. This love for you in My death shows you the extent that I will go to save all souls. I am intent on bringing all of My sheep back home to Heaven. It is by your free will that you choose to love Me. But this time for choosing Me is about to expire. All those, who have chosen to give their life to Me, will lose it and gain Heaven. All those who selfishly refuse to follow My Will will be banished from My kingdom and suffer eternal punishment in Hell."*

Later, at the Mass for Nocturnal Adorers, after Communion, I could see an altar with a large crowd all around it. Jesus said: *"My people, when you come together to receive My Eucharist, you are all united in My One Mystical Body. It is this sharing of My Real Presence that enables Me to help strengthen you with My graces of My Sacrament. Truly, My Eucharistic bread is nourishment for your soul. This is why I tell you that those who eat of My Body and drink of My Blood will have life eternal with Me in Heaven. All of My adorers believe in My Real Presence and are thankful to Me by adoring Me and giving Me praise. I hear your prayers of petition as much as your prayers of thanksgiving. Some faithful only come to Me in their need, but My adorers come frequently just to share in My Presence. Those who truly love Me know that you continually must say how much you love Me or that love will grow cold. For everyone that makes a visit to My Blessed Sacrament, I will reward them with My graces many times over their effort to visit Me. Come and invite others to your places of Perpetual Adoration."*

Wednesday, October 22, 1997:

After Communion, I could see a priest standing at the podium. Jesus said: *"My people, it is truly important to know that to whom more is given, more will be expected. My priests and other Church leaders have been entrusted with the keys of My kingdom and leading the souls of My faithful. That is why they are in deep need of your prayers to fulfill their mission of saving souls. The priests are the caretakers of My sacraments and they are the source of your graces through Me. You still receive the sacraments even if a priest is in sin, yet his morals must be an inspira-*

tion to the faithful. If a priest should mislead souls into sin, this is a serious accounting that he will face at the judgment. It is important to support your priests in their humanity, so there is a good environment for them to succeed. Prophets and lay leaders have the same responsibility not to mislead the faithful. It is important that they be in constant prayer for the direction that the Lord is leading them. Both the priests and lay leaders cannot let pride control them is their positions of authority. Those influencing souls the most must be on the highest moral ground or they will have to answer to My justice. Those who mislead innocent souls will pay a dear price for their misdeeds, but those who bring souls to Me will receive a rich reward in Heaven."

Thursday, October 23, 1997:

After Communion, I could see the Two Tablets of the Ten Commandments coming closer to read. Jesus said: *"My people, see in this vision that you follow My Commandments. It is by these means that you all could lead lives ready for Heaven. In the readings, you can find this same message in 'the wages of sin are death.' When sin controls your life, you are spiritually dead to My love. I have died for you in order to release you from your bondage to sin. Reach out through Confession to have your sins forgiven and be sorrowful that you have offended Me. I am all merciful, and I will welcome you back to a soul full of sanctifying grace when you choose by your free will to be cleansed of your sin. When you return to My love and away from a life of sin, you may experience some resistance both from your body and others around you. You will see this division among your own body and soul, where the spirit clings to Me while the body desires the sinful pleasures. Even among the people around you, when you are cleansed from sin, you will lead new lives which may offend others by your virtues. Your example of prayer to others might challenge their pleasures in sin that some may desire to keep. But do not be discouraged by others' criticism for being good. Your soul is being called to Me, and it may mean that your body may be denied all of its wants and lusts. Show others that through My grace, everyone is called to a higher spiritual life to live above all of your bodily instincts and cravings."*

Later, at the prayer group, I could see a helicopter in a night scene. Jesus said: *"My people, beware of the one world people who are organizing more power in the UN and NATO forces. All of their plans for world control are coming together. Do not fear these men, for they are the ones in danger of losing their souls for consorting with the evil one. My victory will overpower all of their powers and plans, as they do not see My power is always in control."*

I could see some large kettles in a manufacturing place. Jesus said: *"My people, you will see some major events in the coming months. The evil agents of the Antichrist are positioning for his takeover. Corporations and nations will come under increasing control by the one world people. Many jobs will be upset as your standard of living will continually be eroded. Much uncertainty will reign before the Antichrist assumes power."*

I could see in space where some heavenly bodies were moving around. Jesus said: *"My people, you will see many signs in your skies of the coming wars and tribulations. Many will be frightened by some unusual events. Have no fear, My children, for evil will have only a short reign. The Antichrist will perform great signs, but do not believe in him. Worship Me only as I will send My angels to protect your souls."*

I could see a witch and some signs of Halloween. Jesus said: *"My people, do not encourage belief in the evil witches and evil spirits especially around Halloween. There are covens and people who worship Satan all around you in secret. Pray for protection from these forces and do not encourage the children to be like them even in costumes. Some possessions by demons have come through curiosity in these spirits and their symbols."*

I could see a large stage and a huge gold insignia. Jesus said: *"My people, be watchful of the Antichrist's agents who will be organizing large events in stadiums for unsuspecting reasons. His followers will be laying plans for the evil one's entrance into power. Know that as soon as the Antichrist gains control, I will smite his empire with a stroke of My power. Fear not this evil, for its power will be short lived."*

I could see a vision of Mary with her face of purity, and a sense of grace and her presence came over me. Mary said: *"My dear children, just as I have told you of my visits to give the poor souls a respite, so I make many visits to earth to help renew your faith. Many souls have seen many signs of my grace. Do not rely on these brief blessings, for they are only to help you understand Heaven's concern for you. You still will have to suffer in life, but when you pray your Rosaries, my graces will give you spiritual support."*

I could see a spotlight shining down. Jesus said: *"My people, be aware that you are always being seen by the eyes of the world. Your actions are all on display and others will be quick to criticize your misdeeds. If you are to be My ambassadors for the Faith, you must be watching your every move. Live your lives as imitators of My ways. Do not mislead any souls by your bad example. Instead, show all men how you practice what I have taught you, and you are not hypocrites. Follow My commands and demonstrate for all your love for Me and your neighbor."*

Friday, October 24, 1997:

After Communion, I could see a bishop's miter. Jesus said: *"My people, pray for the pope and your bishops, since this time will test all of your Church leaders. There will be many temptations to split with Pope John Paul II. As he is forced to leave Rome, both bishops and priests will have to choose between Pope John Paul II and the Antipope. This new pope will be very appealing to the people, because he will relax many of the Church's positions on tradition. This will begin a major split in My Church with the Antipope controlling all of the churches. My faithful remnant will have to go underground with the faithful priests. That is why all bishops and priests will be tested. Those who are weak will be lost in eventually following the Antichrist. Pray now, My children, for the souls to be properly directed to Me. Believe in My commands and the old traditions of My Church and you will be saved. Those who go along with the schismatic church could lose their souls, if they do not follow Me. You will need My strength and graces to endure this trial."*

At Adoration, I could see some churches and some were in charred ruins. Jesus said: *"My people, when you see some people come to church, there is a strong contradiction from many who are not living their faith. My children, you will see even Church members betray their God by their actions against their neighbor. Many have no answer for what they are doing, except that it is convenient. It is not enough for you to cry 'Lord, Lord,' to be saved. You must witness to My Commandments and seek forgiveness of your sins. Because you go to church, this is no reason to relax your efforts to stop sinning. Because you are close to Me, you should expect more vicious attacks from the evil one. Always be on guard in your actions and seek to avoid temptations. Do not live as hypocrites, so people do not see you leading evil lives. Do not let contradiction be in your life, but show your love for Me and your neighbor is true. Then when you go to church, you will be justified instead of being dishonored. Do not let evil influences destroy your spiritual lives."*

Saturday, October 25, 1997:

After Communion, I could see a few people praying and there was a wave of love that spread out to all those around like a stone thrown in the water. Jesus said: *"My people, in your prayers and good deeds, you do not realize the effect that you have on those around you. Wherever two or more are gathered in My Name, I am there in your midst. Where goodness abounds, My grace can be brought to all you meet through you. Your joy and spirituality is contagious and others will want to partake in your peace and follow Me. On the other hand, where evil abounds, there is hate and anger spread around. So by your prayerful life you can have a spiritually positive atmosphere in your town by encouraging good morals and a love for God. You are called to evangelize and share the love of your Faith with others. My light cannot be held in secret. It must be shared, for My love to move through the world. This is the duty of all My faithful, to spread My love among all the nations."*

Later, at Adoration, I could see some shields with markings on them. Then I could see servicemen of the various branches of the armed forces. Jesus said: *"My people, the reality of the tribulation will be a time of great suffering. There will be some major wars for control of the earth. This is why it is important to pray for peace in the world. As long as man is focused on himself, there will be conflicts over resources, money and land. Man must change his focus to God, if true peace is to be found. True peace of God will only occur through My intervention. Man's conflicts will continue until the devil and his agents are chained in Hell. Man has resisted helps from Heaven's powers to give peace, because he wishes to gain the world's fame and riches for himself only. Strive for My peace and not the tarnished peace of the world. Without My peace, chaos of the evil one will reign over the world."*

Sunday, October 26, 1997:

After Communion, I could see a young adult. (Youth Day) Jesus said: *"My people, as the children get older, they need to have role models in the Faith to follow. They start with their parents or grandparents. They are looking up to you in trust of what to follow in their religious life. This is why it is important that you be good examples of faithful Christians. If you are lax in leading good lives, you will be setting bad examples, and you will be held accountable for your bad influence. Remind your children of their prayers and attending Mass with the sacraments. If you fail to teach the Faith to them, you will be failing your responsibility to bring them up in the Faith. The children will have to choose Me by free will, but you are held accountable for their religious upbringing. Teach them of My love and let them come to Me on Sundays. You are all asked to evangelize souls to Me during life by your Baptism. Go forward to help souls back to Me in any way that you can succeed. When you come to the judgment, do not come with empty hands. For each soul that you bring to Me, your treasure in Heaven will be increased."*

Later, at Adoration, I could see someone at floor level watching a man going behind closed doors. Then there was a global map pictured on the wall. Jesus said: *"My people, I am showing you the signs of secrecy among the workings of the high order of Masons. It is through their power and funding that a lot of these one world controls have come into being. These people have been planning a world takeover for years. These are the ones paving the way for the Antichrist to take control. These one world people, through their funding, have enabled electronics to have the control that it has. My children, fear not their efforts, for they do not realize that their plans are doomed to failure. These men will test your faith, but with My help, you will have the victory over evil. I will send you My angel power to thwart any of their plans. Pray for My protection and you will see miraculous things save you. It is through prayer and My help that you will be able to endure this evil lot. Be assured that My power will reign, and the evil ones will be cast into Hell. All evil will be conquered and the last will be first on the renewed earth."*

Monday, October 27, 1997:

After Communion, I could see four lamp stands at the four corners of the earth. Jesus said: *"My people, I have shown you this vision once before. My four angels are still marking the cross on My faithful at this time. This is the time in Scripture where you are coming close to the time of tribulation. Those who are faithful to Me at this time will suffer, but not nearly the pain of those who refuse Me. Those unfaithful servants will suffer a living Hell of plagues on earth and an eternal punishment in Hell. So come to Me now, My children, while you still have time. I will strengthen My faithful to endure all of the evil one's temptations. Now is the time to prepare for the onslaught of the tribulation. Now will the earth be purified of all evil. You will find My victory just, and My love will reward all those who come to Me in either love or fear of the Lord's wrath."*

Later, I could see some bank robbers robbing a bank and they were wearing black masks. Jesus said: *"My people, beware of man's greed for riches in this world. Many are seeking quick riches, but I have told you not to seek your treasure here on earth. Instead, seek the treasures of My grace in Heaven that no one can steal from you. The things of this world will be stripped from you, so do not be disappointed over this elusive wealth of the world. The monied people of the world have contrived another false move to encourage many to invest in your stock market through artificially low interest rates. Now, they are closing the snare on the people's wealth. If not now, they soon will create a panic or a chaos of events that will make conditions ripe for the takeover by the Antichrist. Many will be seeking peace and stability which the Antichrist will promise. Through man's fears and his seeming miracles, the Antichrist will soon declare himself. This will be your test in faith to remain faithful to Me through all of your tribulation and persecution. Endure this trial but a moment, and I will bring you to the true land of milk and honey in the Era of Peace after My triumph. Be joyous that you are living in this time when you can witness your faith and love in Me despite all of the demon's temptations. I will send My angels soon to gather all the evil into Hell and all My faithful into My barn of spiritual harvest."*

Tuesday, October 28, 1997:

After Communion, I could see a sleek new fighter jet. Jesus said: *"My people, you have grown accustomed to many modern conveniences and a high standard of living. All of these things have come as blessings, but they are all vulnerable. Do not place your trust in the things of this world which can be stripped from you just as easy as you have acquired them. After a storm and your power is taken away, you see how quickly you can meet disaster. So, faith in the advances of science or your money will not help you. Spiritual gains should be your only concern, for it is the soul that is your most valuable possession. Seek to guard it and refresh it through the graces of My sacraments and the protection of My angels. Be more concerned with pleasing Me and following My will than trying to get ahead in the world's riches. These earthly things you cannot take with you, but your resurrection into My glory in Heaven is your soul's most treasured goal."*

Later, at a Healing Mass, I could see a crucifix and then a bright light from a dove of the Holy Spirit. The Holy Spirit said: *"I am the Spirit of God and I am coming to pour My abundant graces upon the people this night. May their souls be open to receive Me, so I can work in their lives. This is always the condition for healing, that you be open in faith to receive a spiritual or physical healing. Many will have their hurts soothed to know that God is watching out for them. Give into the power of My Spirit working in you, and you will be able to fulfill God's Will for you. You are capable of many things in faith, and you restrain the grace working in you, by not trusting that you can accomplish greater things than you are already doing. By understanding the extent of your potential in evangelizing, you will be able to realize more spiritual power that you can perform. God gives you all the gifts that you need. You are the ones that limit His power. So, think beyond human powers, and you will be graced to do the impossible."*

Wednesday, October 29, 1997:

After Communion, I could see someone behind a shield of glass. Jesus said: *"My children, you must come out of your shell of selfishness and pride, so you can open your hearts for Me to enter. By emptying your hearts of self, you can make room for My love to occupy your hearts. Reach out in love both for Me and your neighbor. When you get over your selfish wants and desires, it becomes much clearer how you can help others in their need. Love must be an integral part of your life, or you will fail to come to your spiritual potential. All men and women are made to My image and I am infinite love. If you are to reflect My image, you must make love an everyday part of your life. When you take away these barriers of restraining My love, you become molded in My love to do marvelous acts of mercy, as you store up your treasures in Heaven. Come forward now and receive My loving arms around you, so I can show you how to follow My Will."*

Thursday, October 30, 1997:

After Communion, I could see the Host being raised several times. The white of the Host stood out as the only object that I could focus on. Jesus said: *"My people, listen to the readings today. If you have Me loving you completely, what more do you need? As you are faithful in worshiping Me and following My Will, you will have an everlasting promise to be with Me in Heaven. This is your best retirement plan that anyone could offer you. Because I have paid your ransom from sin, I am freely offering eternal life to you. It is when you die to your own desires of trusting in what you can do, that you open yourself to My loving trust. My love and My Presence to you have shown you My protection in the past, and My help will continue while you are faithful. When you worship Me instead of the world and money, your spiri-*

tual success is guaranteed. You cannot have your eternal life guaranteed from the devil or the world. So come to Me and see that My love is poured out over everyone. All you have to do is allow Me into your heart and I will take care of everything. I offer you a lifetime promise of help. How can you refuse a plan with all of My benefits?"

Later, at the prayer group, I could see some whirling tornadoes and some smoking volcanoes. There were some dark billows of black smoke that could be from oil fires. Jesus said: *"My people, you will continue to see events of chastisement as evil is still controlling many souls. My justice must be answered for the continuing serious sins of abortion and sins of the flesh. Unless you are brought to your knees, many will succumb to the evil one."*

I could see some people in the mines as slave labor. Jesus said: *"My people, you see in the Communist countries how people are forced to work long hours for little pay. The traders of the world and your international corporations want cheap labor to exploit money from the workers. This will be the same trend worldwide as people will have trouble finding jobs with a good wage."*

I could see some classrooms of desks and there were dark demons all over the room. Jesus said: *"My people, beware of what the teachers are teaching the students both in secular classes and religious classes. The demons are encouraging evil teaching to brainwash the children against God. Test what your children and grandchildren are being taught. Do not leave the children in a spiritual vacuum. If they are not taught My love in prayer, they may be influenced by evil intentions."*

I could see some flames and a sense that the lights were out and heat was scarce. Jesus said: *"My people, be prepared this winter for interruptions in your electricity and your fuel to heat your house. With storm events and even forced shortages, you will be severely tested by the cold. Have plenty of blankets and means to keep warm. You will be brought to your knees in prayer until you learn how vulnerable you are to these trials. Pray, My children, that you may change your erring ways."*

I could see Mary come with the saints as they came to Purgatory to give the poor souls a respite of their suffering. Mary said: *"My dear children, rejoice with the saints as you give them honor on their day in glory. At the same time, continue praying dearly for the souls in Purgatory. Many of your relatives may still be suffering these torments. Continue to remember these souls of your relatives and pray for them often. I am giving them the grace of My presence on these feast days. You are called to help these souls as well."*

I could see some prison cells with people in chains. Jesus said: *"My people, you have seen how people have been mistreated by persecution of those in other countries for their faith in God. You will see a gradual persecution mounted against My true remnant in your own country. Be prepared to stand up for your Faith no matter how much you are criticized. All that you suffer for My Name's sake, I will reward you in Heaven and on earth."*

I could see a woman struggling with her small children. Jesus said: *"My people, pray for unity in your families. It is through prayer that you will keep your families together. I draw your attention to reach out and help the single parent mothers who have to struggle in bringing up their children. They need your prayers and your physical help. Reach out to them, since they feel so overwhelmed with expenses and the betrayal of their spouses. They need your loving help, also, since many are starved for someone's love and concern. See to their needs and you will be greatly rewarded."*

Friday, October 31, 1997:

After Communion, I could see a small spotlight. Jesus said: *"My people, you must spread My Gospel of love to all of the peoples of every nation. Your gift of Faith was not given to you just to keep it to yourself. It is freely given, so you may share My love and My gifts to others. Love is contagious, and it has to be shared in order to be expressed. Share My love with all those whom you meet, and do not be afraid to witness your Faith to others. You know how much you treasure those special moments with Me. Why would you not wish that everyone could share such moments? Teach men and women of My love in the Blessed Sacrament. Show them how you reverence My Real Presence. Encourage your friends to know where My Sacred Host is perpetually adored, so they can come visit Me. All of My love needs to be shouted from the rooftops, because it is a message which every-one needs to hear. You have to be My loudspeakers, My hands, and My eyes and ears."*

Later, at Adoration, I could see an earthen home in the side of a hill. Jesus said: *"My people, you worry too much how you are going to provide for yourselves. You need to have more trust in My help for you. You also know of the Antichrist's coming not far off. Do not expect to have places of comfort at all times, espe-cially when you will have to endure trials of the tribulation. You may suffer some inconveniences for a while, but once you come to My Era of Peace, you will experience a joy of My love that you could never have dreamed of. So do not worry about what you will need in the future. Focus on My love and doing My Will and your worries will be over. I will watch and protect My faithful from any evil. With Me bringing you to a land of milk and honey soon, you have all reason to rejoice and trust in Me to provide for your needs."*

Saturday, November 1, 1997: (All Saints' Day)

After Communion, I could see some poor old people walking ahead. Jesus said: *"My people, many times you have heard Me mention that 'the last will be first, and the first will be last.' This is true in life for many who suffer their Purgatory on earth. These are the saints of your day who come to Heaven with many suffer-ings in their hands. Unless you suffer on earth for My Name's sake, you may have to suffer more for your sins in Purgatory. So look on suffering on earth as a blessing, for you will have less stripes to suffer elsewhere for your sins. Those who have suf-fered and were faithful in little things, I have led straight to Heaven, where they have been placed in charge of greater things. It is good for you to see the relationship to those going to Heaven and those going to Purgatory. It is better to suffer here than the flames of purification in Purgatory. Live to be saints now, rather than becoming saints after further purification."*

Later, at St. John's Preparatory School, Danvers, Mass., be-fore the Blessed Sacrament, I could see several vanity tables with mirrors where women prepare themselves. Jesus said: *"My people, you spend time before your mirrors, and you are very concerned about your appearance before others. I, also, am concerned with your appearance, but I am looking into your heart and soul. Many think of the outside more than how they appear to Me on the inside. When you come to adore Me and when you wish to receive Me in Holy Communion, see that you have your inside appearance radiant with My grace. If necessary, you need to frequently come to Me in My Sacrament of Reconciliation, so you can be pleasing to look at on the inside as well as the outside. Also, My children, be more attentive to keeping your interior lives vibrant and not as concerned with your outward beauty. You need to care for the body's needs, but keep your focus on Me in My Blessed Sacrament and not your beauty of self in the mirror."*

Sunday, November 2, 1997: (All Souls' Day)

At Sacred Heart Church, Ipswich, Mass. after Communion, I could see a crucifix among the trees and the yellow leaves were falling to the ground. Jesus said: *"My people, you must die to self to have eternal life with Me. As you see the leaves falling, you see life going through another cycle. You know that unless the seed dies, a new shoot cannot grow. That is why you must die to your own selfish will, so that you can live in the Divine Will. See again, that you are preparing for your death every day. In order to live a Christian life, you must be ready to die for Me. Place yourself in My care and live to imitate My life in all that you do. You are reminded again of your test in the Spirit of what you should do, by following what I would have you do. Be joyful, My friends, that you have this glorious life to live for Me every glorious day that you live. Give thanks to Me for My love, and return My love in your love for Me and your neighbor."*

Later, at St. John's Preparatory School, Danvers, Mass., I could see a fence overlooking a raging river. Jesus said: *"My people, again you are seeing some flooding of rivers which will continue in your country, since many are not heeding My calls. I have pleaded with you many times to come to your senses, concerning your many sins. Your chastisements through your weather will continue and many will suffer great losses. See in these storms a double-edged sword. On one side, your blessings in material things will be stripped from you. In a spiritual way, your sins will be cleansed by these waters as well. When you suffer from these hardships, it is My way of showing you what is important and what is not. You will see that you can get along without your possessions, but you cannot get along without Me. I am your Bread of Life and you need My nourishment for your souls to find its way to Heaven. Rejoice even in your hardships, for it will direct you more to Me than the temptations of the world."*

Monday, November 3, 1997:

After Communion, I could see a corner of a wall and then looking around it, I could see a new event occurring. Jesus said: *"My people, do not be curious about the timing of future events. I foresee into the future and I know of the events to come. I have conveyed this information to the prophets of Scripture and to some of My messengers. I only give you warnings of things to come when it is necessary for your soul to know. But do not be anxious to know details of the future that are not necessary for you to know. Those things foretold in the Scriptures have yet to be fulfilled, but they are not long away in reference to the time of your tribulation. I will allow this short time of testing from this evil one, to see if you will have faith enough in Me, to let Me lead you to safety. My loving arms are always protecting My faithful. Why would you doubt that I would leave you alone in this trial? Trust in My help and do not think that you could survive this evil alone."*

Later, at Adoration, I could see a small altar set up in a home for Mass. Then I saw some churches with money coming out of the doors. Jesus said: *"My people, it is time to prepare now for your underground Masses. Go now and obtain all of the vessels, vestments and books to say Mass. Stock up on your bread and wine. There is coming a time very shortly when you will no longer have your churches for Mass. The schismatic church will take them over and soon there will no longer be any valid Masses there. You will need to find a faithful priest for a true Mass of My Real Presence. You will have to preserve and guard My Consecrated Hosts from the evil ones who will desire them to desecrate. I will be close to you during this persecution. Call on Me for Spiritual Communion when you cannot get to a valid Mass. I love you, My people. Remain faithful to Me even if you must suffer for My Name's sake."*

Tuesday, November 4, 1997:

After Communion, I could see a strong white light at the end of a tunnel. Jesus said: *"My people, I am the Light of the World and I draw all men to Me. As in today's Gospel, My call goes out to everyone, but many have refused to come. Those who refuse to respect Me will never taste of My dinner. The Bread of Heaven will only be given to My faithful. I send out My beacon of light as a hope for all the lost souls. I am always in search of your souls until your dying day. I wait even until the eleventh hour for all souls to seek My love and glory. Then at the end of your life, all the souls are called to judgment before Me. At that time, all knees must bend to Me as you are brought through the tunnel of death. As you are directed to My Light, come to Me with your heavenly treasures, for they will be your witness of faith before Me."*

Later, at Adoration, I could see an old radio in a wooden case. Jesus said: *"My people, over the years you have seen a dramatic increase in knowledge, which is one of the signs of the end times. Another observation is how many of your inventions are helping the evil one to spread sin. You have television, movies, and magazines to spread pornography. Your communications are being abused to shape man's minds to desire worldly things. With the microchips, Internet and satellites there is room for the evil one to control your mind by subliminal ads and desires for the lust of pleasure. My friends, take a look around you and do not be influenced by these evil desires. You may find it easier to live a holy life, if you were to avoid all of these electronic gadgets. By withdrawing from the temptations of these influences, your soul may be protected from the evil one's attacks from these sources. Think how you could be more constructive with your time by not letting these devices control your mind. I love you and I desire you to expand your thinking on how to please Me more in your life. You will see a step forward in your spirituality when you disengage your life from electrical devices."*

Wednesday, November 5, 1997:

After Communion, I could see a horizontal view of fire or light and the upper sky was dark or black. Jesus said: *"My people, what I am showing you is at the beginning of the Three Days of Dark-*

ness. After the comet strikes, there will be massive volcanic activity. You will initially see the fire of the volcanoes on the horizon. As much dust and ash will be released into the air, then the sun will be completely blotted out. It is at this time that you need to be inside and not looking at the lost souls who will be burning in a living Hell on earth. Only blessed candles will give light at that time. Have faith that I will protect My faithful during this cataclysm. After the plagues of revelation are over, I will chain Satan, his demons and all the evil people in Hell. Then the renewal of the earth will take place, and I will bring My faithful back to a renewed earth as the Era of Peace will begin. Rejoice, My people, for those living at this time will enjoy paradise on earth as Adam experienced."

Thursday, November 6, 1997:

After Communion, I could see two Christmas trees spinning, and then they came to a stop. Jesus said: *"My people, many of you are in a blur of activity in preparing gifts and your decorations for Christmas. Your time disappears so fast with your activity, that you are there at My feast day before you realize it. This year, you need to slow down your lifestyle, so you can prepare properly for this glorious season. The readings and Advent are a time to prepare your souls for My coming at Christmas. Prepare your hearts and keep your charity and love for each other in focus. Christmas is a time of joy and peace, so do not be so wrapped up in the preparations, that you miss the spirit of this time."*

Later, at the prayer group, I could see an old church and a smaller church was inside it. Jesus said: *"My people, this smaller church represents My holy remnant who are always faithful to Me. See that many are called, but few are chosen. There is another meaning to this vision as of the House of Loreto. My friends, follow the imitation of the Holy Family. Live in your families with prayer always guiding you."*

I could see some documents sitting on a table in an interrogation room. Jesus said: *"My people, if you should be imprisoned for My Name's sake, remain faithful at all times. They will try to torture you into signing documents that deny Me. Even if you must die for your beliefs, have faith and trust that I will guard your soul.*"

I could see a woman dressed in traditional ethnic clothes. Jesus said: "*My people, do not worry if people criticize your religious beliefs as being old-fashioned and not modern. Hold fast to your roots in My Catholic Church led by Pope John Paul II. Never give up the teaching that I have given you from My Apostles. Many false witnesses will try to change My Church in the name of reform, but they really mean to destroy My Church. Be aware of the apostasy against Me, and never turn your back on Me.*"

I could see a bright light leading to a church. Mary came and said: "*My dear children, thank you for your Rosaries this night. Even though you may have to move about in your prayer groups, remain faithful in your prayers that you pray together. You will find spiritual strength in your prayer groups to support you in these coming trials. It is good to keep close, so that you can help each other in your needs.*"

I could see some dark alleyways with single lightbulbs as in the Old Jerusalem. Jesus said: "*My people, over the years man has not changed much in his craving to possess things. The rich always lord it over the poor. The rich still desire to control the world, and they will even make pacts with the devil to obtain their desires. That is why the Middle East will always be in turmoil over the control of the land. Beware of these wars of ownership. Have nothing to do with them.*"

I could see a trash can. Jesus said: "*My people, look at things that you keep and the things that you throw away. When you have a finite space, you have to set priorities on what to keep. So it is in your souls. You have a space for you or Me. You must empty yourself of your selfish desires and then allow Me to enter and occupy your thoughts. If you refuse to let Me in, then you may be hanging on to your excess baggage of the world. Free yourself of the world by opening your hearts to follow My Will.*"

I could see President Clinton and the Chinese Premier at some meetings. Jesus said: "*My people, pray for your leaders that they seek Me and not more power and fame. Beware of the evil one's influence on your leaders to cause wars in trade or combat. The Antichrist is coming soon, and he will exploit these men as pup-*

pets for his own control. Once he has what he wants, he will do away with any of their power. See now how your leaders are even now plotting for a takeover. Have faith in My help, for the worldly things will be taken away from you. You will have to trust in Me fully for everything. Be willing to submit to My will and I will bring you through all of these trials."

Friday, November 7, 1997:

After Communion, I could see some places in church and a black demon blotted out one seat with darkness. Jesus said: *"My people, you need to be more conscious of the demons working in your churches. Many are being deceived in what to believe. Changes being made in the Mass will soon threaten My very Presence in the Mass. Satan will strike at My priests, and he will encourage the schismatic church. Be aware that there are many divisions in My Church which are threatening to break away from My Pope John Paul II. Pray for the priests and the people, when this split will be coming. My faithful need to stay strong in your prayer groups, because your testing is about to begin. I am again warning you to see the hand of the evil one in all of this unbelief. Stay true to My Words of Scripture and I will always protect you."*

Later, at Adoration, I could see a British flag briefly, and then a flag of orange dots on a black background took its place. Jesus said: *"Yes, My friends, England will play a part in the coming of the Antichrist. There are some monied connections that the Antichrist will take advantage of. England is a central nation in the European Common Market. Watch for the moves that England takes as men prepare for the Antichrist's announcement of his coming to power."*

Saturday, November 8, 1997:

After Communion, I could see an election booth at the voting polls. Jesus said: *"My people, you have just recently voted for your secular leaders at the voting booth. You are always told how important that each vote is, especially in close elections. I tell you, it is also important whom you choose for your spiritual leader — Satan or Me. As in the readings, you cannot have two masters. You will love one and hate the other. You have been blessed with free will to choose whom you wish to love. I do not force My love on anyone, but I offer it freely, since I am Infinite Love. So, My friends, choose life, since you will either follow Satan and the world, or you can follow Me to eternal life in Heaven. Count the costs versus the rewards. If you choose to follow Satan, you may have money and human pleasures for awhile, but look at the cost of going to Hell for an eternity of pain in flames. If you choose to follow Me, you may suffer some pain on earth for My Name's sake, but your reward in My peace and My love in Heaven for eternity has no comparison in value. Choose the one who created you, for I have provided all that your soul could ever desire. I am the goal of your soul, since you were made to praise and adore Me as the angels. It is only by foolish pride that you would ever reject Me. So, after weighing each side, you will realize all that I offer cannot be refused, either by logic or by love. All I ask is to see if Satan and the world loves you like I do. Come to the One who truly loves you and does everything for you. Satan hates and despises man. He is not helping you at all."*

Later, at Jerry Segrue's wedding at St. Paul's Church, Webster, after Communion, I could see a large beautiful cathedral and a bride was in view. Jesus said: *"My dear children, you are My bride and I am your spouse. Weddings are a beautiful time to enkindle My love in your hearts. This is a perfect model to show you how much I love you, since you know of human love. Listen to the words of seeking the higher gifts of love and praise. You think more of earthly things, at times, because of your weakened condition. But when you seek heavenly things, it requires a love from the heart. Your soul always yearns for a higher spiritual calling. That is why you feel so incomplete with only earthly things. Satisfy your souls' desire by receiving Me in the sacraments. There is a great grace that I grant to all newlyweds to love each other with an unconditional love. By praying together in your marriage, you can seal your love with My Infinite Love. In this way, your faith in Me and your spouse will be more permanent."*

Sunday, November 9, 1997: (St. John Lateran Dedication)
After Communion, I could see a graveyard and some demons and then a church. Jesus said: *"My people, I have given the Keys*

of Heaven to St. Peter and his successors, and the Gates of Hell shall not prevail against it. It is My Presence in the Host of the tabernacles that makes My churches holy. At each dedication, I bless each church by having My angels protect them. You are in an age when only a few give proper respect to My Real Presence in the Host. I am still present whether people believe or not. You may be called on to protect My Hosts from desecration by the evil ones. Preserve My Blessed Sacrament and the proper consecration of the bread at Mass. It is only by passing this heritage on to your younger generations that you will keep My Real Presence among you. Pray for the priests that they will be loyal to reverence My Blessed Sacrament and to saying the Mass properly for the sake of My faithful. When the schism strikes My Church, many of My lambs will be scattered. Pray for strength at that time, so your angels will guide you to a proper Mass."

Later, at Adoration, I could see a Marian display of statues, Miraculous Medals, scapulars, Rosaries and prayer cards for novenas. Mary said: *"My dear children, do not be so worried about having enough of this world's things to live on. If you follow my Son's Will, He will provide for all of your needs. I am showing you all of these sacramentals that you will need for your spiritual protection. Your soul is much more important than the body. So, focus first on my protection of my scapular and my Rosary. These are your weapons against Satan. Other protections are holy water, your Crosses and your Bibles. With my Son and I wrapping our arms around you, you have the best assurance that the evil one will not get to your soul. My Son and I are protecting the faithful daily in your struggles to save souls. Take time out to always help souls to come closer to us, and pray for their spiritual and physical needs. With your help, you can lead many souls to their salvation. This gift of yourself will be most rewarded."*

Monday, November 10, 1997:

After Communion, I could see some corn rotting away to nothing. Jesus said: *"My people, you pride yourself on your abundance of goods. Do not rely on this earthly wealth, for it can rot and dissipate tomorrow. Even your food that you thought you had enough of, will rot before your eyes, leaving you close to famine. Food will become more of a scarcity because of your weather and the control of the one world people. Your food will become higher priced, and it will be used as blackmail by the Antichrist and his agents. This is how the Mark of the Beast and the smart cards will attract many unsuspecting victims who would not listen to My advice. Remain faithful to Me despite this change in events, for I will provide your food and shelter. Many would rather trust in their own means than following My Will. My faithful realize that I will endure over all odds to save you. Worship Me only and you will feast at My banquet."*

Later, at Adoration, I could see some men giving orders over the television. Jesus said: *"My people, beware of the power of the airwaves and your cable through your television. This will truly be a means of the Antichrist to reach many people with a deceptive message of his peace. Many are already habitual watchers. Your craving for news and your curiosity have drawn many to believe everything said in your news. There is much deception in your media. You only receive information that the ones in power want you to hear. Those things of the one world people are kept secret. So it will be when the Antichrist will declare himself. He will use miraculous powers to persuade many to worship him, as an answer to all of man's problems. Before he comes into power, you must disconnect yourself from radio, television, cable, and the Internet. Otherwise, the evil one's net will brainwash you into worshiping this false christ. Unless you rely on My help, you will surely be lost. I send your guardian angels to protect you. Keep faithful to Me in all of these trials, and you will enjoy My day in the coming Era of Peace."*

Tuesday, November 11, 1997:

After Communion, I could see a snake traveling on the water. Jesus said: *"My people, this vision shows you the serpent as a representation of the Devil. He is cunning and strikes to bite all of mankind with his fangs of the world. He spews his poison into all the hearts of man by his temptations. You are to be on guard as a soldier, because you know not how he will strike at you. Prepare yourself with prayer and your blessed sacramentals. The demons will have more power in this era, but I give you My angels for protection. The more you follow My Will in faith, the stronger you will be in standing up to the Devil's temptations. Always be aware of his presence, so you can keep your guard up for his ploys. Trust in My help to guard your souls, and you shall have no fear of evil."*

At Adoration, I could see some flames and then a large graveyard. Jesus said: *"My people, I am reminding you of the flames of Hell and of when everyone has to die. Many plan for everything except where they are going after death. You think that you are in control of your life, until you see around you how people are surprised when they die. No matter how much you plan to be comfortable, all of you will have to experience pain and death. Since your soul is immortal, you should be concerned more how you are going to spend eternity instead of just the few years that you spend here. Living your life for Me will put you on the right course to Heaven. There is more to life than just pleasures and money. Gaining Heaven should be everyone's top priority. To be with Me in Heaven means that you are willing to give everything up for Me. You cannot love money and Me at the same time. If I am your Lord, then you are to love Me and your neighbor. Pile up your wealth in good deeds in Heaven, and you will have more to show for your life than piled up riches in the world. You cannot take your money with you, so think more of how you can please Me in what you do. Set your focus on Me and you will have all that you need."*

Wednesday, November 12, 1997:

After Communion, I could see a pathway forward and a sense of the holidays was around me. Jesus said: *"My people, the readings today talk of giving thanks to God for My gift of healing the lepers. This is in keeping with the spirit of your feast of Thanksgiving. Many, even today, take for granted My gifts of jobs, health, faith and even life itself. It takes a gracious heart to give a thank you either to Me or your neighbor. It also takes a denial of pride to admit that you alone are not responsible for all of your good fortune. Those who have committed their lives to Me, never worry about any pain or struggles that they must endure. It is more important to do these things out of love, than worry about being repaid for your service. Those willing to go that extra mile for Me and your neighbor, are to be thanked for their graciousness as well. Many fail to realize that unless many of their gifts were given to them, they would not succeed in anything. I do not demand your thanks, because when you give thanks by your own free will, it shows your growth in your spirituality. Be examples to others in giving Me credit for doing things, instead of bragging of your own success."*

Thursday, November 13, 1997: (Mother Cabrini)

After Communion, I could see Mother Cabrini dressed in black and she said: *"My children, look to all souls as Jesus looks upon them with compassion and love. Our Lord never refuses to help us in all that we do. We must be imitators of that love and reach outside of ourselves in helping others. It is your corporal works of mercy that you must have in your hands when you come before God. Since you have helped His little ones in any way, you have helped to love Him. When you do things out of love, not worrying about your time or expense, then you are acting in God's image in you. All of you may not be able to follow all that I did, but even if you try in a small way to help your brother, you will find your reward in Heaven."*

Later, at the prayer group, I could see a large church with an old window and a priest wearing a biretta. Jesus said: *"My dear people, you have been graced with a faith and a tradition which was passed on to you through the Apostles. Be faithful to your Pope John Paul II in all of his teachings. He is directing you to Heaven by his writings. You will see various clergy try to split My Church from its tradition and My teachings. Pray for discernment and do not be misled in your faith."*

I could see some computer disks as CD-ROMS. Jesus said: *"My people, many souls are being seduced into spending many hours on your computers. You, yourself, know the pitfalls of letting computers run your lives. These devices can be a source of abuse and a god with a little 'g' for some. Do not spend so much time on such frivolities. You need to be more in prayer and following My Will instead of pleasure-seeking."*

I could see some Arabs and they were on thrones, but they were in the dark. Jesus said: *"My people, there are some of these Arabs who are working with the forces of the dark side. They mislead many into wars of hate for its own sake, because they are inspired by Satan in their hearts. Be forewarned of the activities of certain defiant factions against many of your nations. If others follow them, they could rouse the people into more serious wars. Pray again for peace in this area of the Mid-East, for the clouds of Armageddon are gathering on the horizon."*

I could see the leaves falling, as I looked through a door on a house and preparations were being made for winter. Jesus said: *"My people, your weather events are about to begin. This will be a winter season to remember when you will look back on this time. Your storms will intensify as nature will unleash its fury on you. Your chastisements will continue as many are not taking My messages of love and warning to heart. I have asked My faithful to prepare for these events."*

I could see some construction equipment and building supplies of metal sheets. Jesus said: *"My people, do not be surprised when you see more detention centers being constructed. The one world people will try to imprison you in their death camps. Flee into hiding before they come for you. Your troops are being cut back and dispersed by wars of distraction. You will have no one to protect you from the UN occupation forces. Seek My help, and do not take up weapons in the battle of good and evil."*

I could see Mary come dressed in white on some clouds. Mary said: *"My dear children, soon you will be celebrating some of my feast days, as well as preparing again for my Son at His commemoration at Christmas. These days are short before His real coming again as well. Always be in preparation to receive my Son into your hearts. You never know of the day of His coming, so come to Him in the sacraments, so you can have your souls in a state of grace. Frequent your confessionals, especially as these feasts approach you."*

I could see some tents draped in white as outdoor temporary hospital wards. Jesus said: *"My people, man will be making his own plagues over the earth, as a result of his experiments with biological weapons. Some of these plagues and your nuclear devices will cause great devastation in lives throughout the world. The one world people have unleashed a sickness which will be uncontrolled, and many will die as a result."*

Friday, November 14, 1997:

After Communion, I could see a large winter snowfall being plowed away. Jesus said: *"My people, you make preparations for winter, but you never know when these storms will come. Those who are not ready have difficulty in getting around. So it was with Noah and Sodom and Gomorrah. My faithful were prepared, but the sinful people did not want to believe these things could happen. You, My people, are being warned as well to make ready for My Second Coming. You, also, do not know the day, but I am giving you the warning to prepare, for it is not far away. Have your souls free from sin by frequent Confession, and you will have no worries of when I will come. Again, woe to those who live in wanton pleasure and sin, for a day will come when they are not suspecting, and they will be hurled into Hell with a sudden judgment. My Scriptures are there to read. Heed My Words or you will be doomed to repeat the condemnation of those evil people in the past. My justice will be swift, but for those who listen to My Words, My mercy will abound."*

Later, at Adoration, I could see some military vehicles traveling at night on the road in a convoy. Jesus said: *"My people, both your country and Iraq are preparing for war in your troop movements. Pray, My people, for peace in your world. Do not be fighting over pride. There is much hatred which forms during war, and there are never any winners. These wars to satisfy men's egos are uselessly spending innocent lives. Be aware when all of your troops are away from home, for you will be left vulnerable for takeover. These will be the devious tactics of the one world people to bog you down in such fruitless wars with threats over oil. You would be better to stay at peace, than to appease your power hungry leaders. Again, pray that these incidents will be settled without loss of life."*

Saturday, November 15, 1997:

After Communion, I could see a mailbox by the road. Jesus said: *"My people, I am showing you this mailbox because you send your prayers to Me as love letters. When you pray your petitions, your praise, or for whatever reason you pray to Me, I am always listening. When you pray, let it come from your heart and soul and not just words. Pray with meaning, not just out of habit or duty, but with fervor and true contrition in your sorrow for sin. Another prayer I ask you not to forget, are prayers of thanksgiving for all the many gifts that you have been given. Your life is*

full of reasons for prayer, and it is a beautiful way for the soul to keep in touch with Me and focused on your spiritual communication. In addition to prayer formally, your informal prayer throughout the day is also a way to keep Me in focus. Offer up all of your day's activities as a prayer to Me, and all that you do will be blessed. By keeping close to Me in prayer while you have spare time, it will thwart the enemy in distracting you into sin. Even pray for My help in temptation to keep your life holy."

Later, at Spiritus Sanctus School (Domino Pizza Headquarters) Ann Arbor, Mich. at Adoration I could see some furniture in a classroom and then a child appeared. Jesus said: *"My people, you are concerned in having your children taught well in the secular schools. Even more, you must remember that with children, you are dealing with souls which have to answer to Me in their lives. It is even more important, therefore, that you concern yourself with the religious education of your children. Many of My older faithful remember how they were given the Faith through the nuns. It is even more important now that you teach your children the true Catholic Faith that comes from the Apostles. It is your responsibility as parents of these souls who are entrusted to your spiritual care. So, I ask you to encourage all benefactors and teachers to continue this effort in passing on the Faith to your children. These same people will receive a rich reward in Heaven for all the souls that are brought to Me. Your faith does not have any monetary value, but in Heaven it is priceless."*

At Immaculate Queen of Heaven & Earth Prayer Group in Ann Arbor, Mich. during the Rosary I had a pain in my shoulder, and I had a vision of Jesus carrying His Cross. Jesus said: *"My people, you must learn to offer up all of your sufferings to Me and take up your daily cross. Many frown on pain and do everything to alleviate pain. My faithful, you must see My sufferings are an example for you on earth. There is merit in your suffering when you offer it up in atonement for your sins and those of others. If you could suffer your Purgatory here, you could save the grievous pain of flames later. If you complain now of a little pain, how will you suffer the cleansing flames of Purgatory. Use your prayer groups to pray for each other and the lost sinners. Many waste their pain when it could be used for so much good. So, look on your pains in a spiritual light as blessings to make you humble and not complainers."*

Sunday, November 16, 1997:

At St. Thomas More Church, Troy, Mich. after Communion, I could see through a round magnifying glass very clearly to read some print. Jesus said: *"My people, I am showing you in this magnifying glass how the eyes of faith can make everything spiritually clear. As you look at things through the eyes of the world, only greed for money and possessions are seen with no element of the supernatural. Given the gift of faith, creation and love add a bigger dimension to life. When you think with the eyes of faith, your obligations and responsibilities are enhanced as well. By faith you see how living by My Will, all of these necessities of life will be granted to you. You are asked to love Me and your neighbor in a way that takes self-will out of the picture. When you live to please Me, you will be called to help each other lovingly and not looking for any personal gain. This life of love comes with growth in your spirituality. So pray, My children, that you need to appreciate your tasks that I am asking you to do in faith. The more that you trust in My help, the more work for souls I will be able to do through you. Remain open to My love and your reward will far outweigh any test of your endurance."*

Monday, November 17, 1997:

After Communion, I could see a baseball field. Jesus said: *"My people, a baseball player has several chances to get a hit during a game. You also have many opportunities for conversion. Each day of your life is another chance to accept Me as Lord of your life. But just as a game has a finite number of innings, you too have only so long to come to Me. You must seek My grace for help in overcoming your evil ways. Have faith as the blind man in the readings that you can be healed. Your spiritual healing is more important than any earthly healing. Be open to My help, and beautiful things will happen in your life."*

Later, at Adoration, I could see some people in a festive mood preparing baskets for the poor. Jesus said: *"My people, every year at this time there is a great rush of emotion to give thanks by helping the poor with a Thanksgiving meal. It is good for you to think of helping others, but you may want to go one step further and carry this spirit throughout the whole year. Many of you give from your excess money, but remember how I marveled at the widow's mite of all that she had. You are here only a short time. So, do not spend that time piling up money only for yourself, but give even more of yourself to help others in your time and your money. Those who are gracious will have many treasures stored up in Heaven. There are many saints who have given up even all of their wealth to be fully dependent on Me. So, be gracious at this time and as often as you can, since your love can be shared with so many, if you would just open your heart."*

Tuesday, November 18, 1997:

After Communion, I could see from above a large metal netted waste basket. Jesus said: *"My people, it is no accident that corporate America is decimating its workforce. Your economy is booming, and yet your corporations are acting as if they were in major recession. It is really the greed of their stockholders who are telling the executives that the people who work for them are dispensable. I have told you that your standard of living will drop and your possessions will be stripped from you. This will be happening both through chastisements and the manipulation of the one world people who want you to be less independent and more dependent on them. By stripping your benefits and removing the factory jobs, many will hold on to a bare existence. Many of your blessings are being stripped away as a consequence of your apathy to your sins. The additional reason is to make more people easier to be controlled by the coming of the Antichrist. You are seeing a battle of good and evil, and many people will be displaced in the upheaval of this age. Pray, My people, as you will need spiritual strength to face all kinds of trials in this battle for souls."*

Later, at Adoration, I could see a large stage with huge markings on the curtain. Then I saw some strange red laser lights which were bent in odd shapes. Jesus said: *"My people, soon the Antichrist and his agents will be making some announcements of his preparations. Whenever he will appear, there will be great signs and wonders to those watching. By his illusions and his powers, he will convince some unsuspecting souls that he is the man to bring peace to the earth. By these manifestations some will believe that he is sent from God. He will claim to be Me, but do not be deceived into believing him. The Antichrist's powers will draw many to follow him. I am showing you that My power will overcome him. He will only be allowed a set time when you will know of his reign. As soon as he gains power over the earth, I will come to vanquish him in the final Battle of Armageddon. Keep away from his influence and travel with the protection of your sacramentals."*

Wednesday, November 19, 1997:

After Communion, I could see a priest returning the Hosts to the tabernacle. Jesus said: *"My people, you are fortunate each day that you have an opportunity to receive Me in Holy Communion. If you*

can receive Me each day, why not take advantage of My graces and My help in this sacrament? It is true that a day is coming when you may no longer have this grace at your disposal. You will have to seek Me then in Spiritual Communion. My Real Presence needs to be taught more to the people. Those who become aware of My miracles of the Eucharist have no doubt and have their faith enhanced. Learn that it is in My Presence that you are given My power of grace. Seek Me in Adoration and give Me praise that I allow you to visit Me in the Holy Bread."

Thursday, November 20, 1997:

After Communion, I could see a picture of the Antichrist in an ornate gold frame and everyone was made to worship it. Jesus said:

"My people, it will soon be upon you to choose whether or not to worship the image of the beast. If you do worship it, you will receive great praise and wealth from the world. If you do not, you will be doomed to be an outlaw forever. Those who worship Me only will be like those in the readings today. I am not calling you to kill anyone or take up armaments, but you will be called on to give up all of your possessions and go into hiding. Those who wish to be openly defiant and become martyrs will have their opportunity to defy the Antichrist. When those who are defiant come forward, do not look on the Antichrist or his image, for there will be power there to cause you to worship him. Instead, pray to Me for strength to endure these evil people for a short time. I will soon destroy this lot and their last state of their souls will be worse than the first."

Later, at the prayer group, I could see some pictures of relatives and a woman looking at them. Jesus said: *"My people, this is a beautiful time when families get together to share a holiday meal. For some it is a time of joy, for others there is a loneliness of separation. Those who can help should share their holiday with those who are alone or sick. Be always considerate of all of your family members, especially, those who are having bad feelings with each other. In all of your festivities, be thankful to God for all that you have."*

I could see some small chips ready to be placed in the hand. Jesus said: *"My people, your time is coming soon when you will have to decide about taking the chip of the beast or not. It will first come in your smart cards and then proceed into people's hands. Those who refuse these chips will be tested and you will need to seek My help and protection. Do not take the smart card or the same chip in the hand. This will allow the Antichrist to control you."*

I could see in Egypt a vision of the Sphinx and the pyramids. Jesus said: *"My people, this terrorism will continue as militant groups, led by the one world, will try to create chaos. This disruption of the peace will lead to a call for a world police state which will eventually make way for the Antichrist. See that all of these atrocities, wars and rumors of wars, will bring you to the great tribulation."*

I could see some very clear pictures displayed on a TV. Jesus said: *"My people, your new technology will be deceiving. There will be two-way listening in many of these devices to spy on you in your homes. These new machines will be used by the Antichrist to get people to worship him. Avoid these new systems, for they will be devious and cunning in their influence. As time approaches the tribulation, do away with all of your electronic communications."*

I could see a dark church and then a gold icon of Mary. Mary said: *"My dear children, continue praying your Rosaries, for this is your great weapon against Satan and his agents. The time of your testing is not far away, but you should glory in the promise of my Son's Second Coming. As you prepare for Christmas, keep my Son's coming in glory uppermost in your mind. The joy of our triumph far surpasses any trials that you may suffer. The more you come together in your prayer groups, the stronger you will all be in your faith. You will be tested, but my mantle will be ever protecting you."*

I could see some nuns in their habits. Jesus said: *"My people, your priests and sisters are being put to the test more than ever by the evil one. Some are being tested with the things of the world, and others by pride in their allegiance to their superiors. Both the religious and the laity must be under obedience to My Will. It is following in My footsteps that the priests are called to witness. Pray for the priests and the nuns who are struggling with their identity."*

I could see the Sacred Heart of Jesus flaming with His Love and His Light which cast a golden glow on His heart. Jesus said: *"My dear children, My love goes out to all of you that are suffering in your troubles. Life has its joys and sorrows, so you must always be ready to accept the challenges that you will receive. It is your suffering that will test the depth of your faith. I give you many gifts to endure your trials. Just come to Me for your help. Do not be saddened by discomforts, but see that they help you to grow in your faith. Live to follow Me in good times and bad, and you will see My love for you endures forever. With Me always with you, who could stand against you?"*

Friday, November 21, 1997:

After Communion, I could see a door to a prison with bars on it. Jesus said: *"My people, you have seen My own people imprison Me as a thief. I preached the coming of My Kingdom, but they refused to believe in My miracles. Many concern themselves too much with worldly affairs. It is following Me through the persecution for My Name's sake that I ask of each of My disciples. I have suffered much in going before you. Be prepared to suffer much from the world. They will hate you as they did Me. Despite all of man's threats, you are to love everyone, even your persecutors. In that way you will heap hot coals of love upon their heads and they will be confounded. The world considers you a fool for Me, but you are spiritually wise in My ways. Continue to carry your cross, so you can await your heavenly crown of victory with Me."*

Saturday, November 22, 1997:

At St. Augustine's Church in Tuscon, Arizona after Communion, I could see a dawn on the hills and mountains. There was a majestic coming of Jesus in the clouds as ruler of the earth. Jesus said: *"My dear children, you are preparing for My great feast of My Kingship. No matter what each person believes, everyone's knee must bend in adoration of Me, for I am the Almighty. Nothing happens without My approval. No matter how much you think that evil is in control, remember that I am only allowing this for a time. As in the Gospel, I allow the wheat to grow with the tares. But a time is coming when I will call down My angels to separate the evil ones from My faithful. The good will come into My barn of everlasting life, while the Devil and the evil ones will be cast into the flames of Hell. Heed My words, a day is coming when you least suspect. Be at peace, My little ones, by being in My grace through Confession. Be prepared to receive your Master and you will have no fear. I pour My love out over all of you. Come to Me and share My rest."*

Sunday, November 23, 1997:

At St. Jerome's Church in Phoenix, Arizona after Communion, I could see a darkened enclosure as a world in sin. Then Jesus came on the clouds of glory and He descended on the earth. The children

were all around Him. Jesus said: *"My children, I come this day to show you that I am King of the Universe. This is the feast that all of you are preparing for, My Second Coming. I will come on the clouds as the angels told you how I would return. My glory and My power will go out all over the earth as Satan will be conquered and chained in Hell. This triumph that I will establish on the earth, will show you My kingdom on earth. All humanity has awaited My Second Coming since I last ascended into Heaven. At this triumph every knee shall bend, as My judgment will rule. My love will be poured out all over My faithful while all those evil men will be cast into Hell. There will be no doubt as I arrive in glory that I am all powerful, and no one will be able to stand up to Me, even Satan. My rule in My kingdom will be all pervading as Heaven will rejoice in My victory over evil. Come, My faithful, as you will soon share in My banquet table."*

Monday, November 24, 1997:

At St. Jerome's Church in Phoenix, Arizona after Communion, I could see a cross on a wall with a light shining on it. Jesus said: *"My people, remember to take up your cross each day and carry it for My Name's sake. You have good experiences and the valleys of difficult times. You need to bear all that has been given to you with a joyful heart. Think of your duty in working for Me as an honor to be able to express your love and giving of yourself to Me. You all have been gifted with an opportunity to serve Me in faith. Those who have accepted My call to salvation have the richest prize of all. By doing good works and following My commands, you will be richly rewarded with a treasure in Heaven no one can take from you. So, each morning in your prayers, direct your lives of service with a bond to Me that is a pleasure for you to follow."*

Later, at Adoration, I could see someone making Christmas cookies. Jesus said: *"My people, the Advent Season will soon be upon you in your preparation for My feast at Christmas. This is another feast in the Church when many Catholics feel drawn to come to church. Christmas is My gift of love to you when I first came into the world. This is a time when you can bring your gift of love to Me. There are so many symbols in faith associated with*

55

this feast day. My coming will bring you My light in the darkness of your sins. Your gifts of love can be just like the gifts given to Me by the Magi. My star even shows you the way that you can follow Me. This entry into human life was the first step in bringing all of you the salvation I promised all men. So, give praise and glory to Me as the angels, and you will be filled with My peace and love."

Tuesday, November 25, 1997:

After Communion, I could see some fine marble palaces and they were all crumbling to dust. Jesus said: *"My people, what you have read about these ancient kingdoms crumbling, will be happening again with the kingdoms of this age. Man's greed and his sins are causing his structures to crack and fall under their own weight of evil. Even now, you are seeing financial and physical cracks in many countries about to be toppled. There is no longer a desire to trust in Me in holding up even your own nation. When man relies only on himself, he is doomed to failure. Evil men in your government will bring you to your own demise. These evil men will not last long either, since My purification will soon hurl them to their fiery judgment in Hell. Look at the readings today as a picture of the future. The Antichrist will take over all of the nations, but just as he feels that he has won, My victory will triumph and his kingdom will fall to pieces. Look to Me, My people, and be saved, for I will provide My protection through My angels. Be persistent in your allegiance to Me, and I will raise you to higher things even on this earth."*

Later, at the prayer group in St. Cecilia's Church, I could see frogs and rats running in groups. Jesus said: *"My people, there will be many plagues called down on the earth as the seals are broken over those who are unfaithful to Me. These plagues will spread disease and pestilence. My faithful will be protected as the angel passed over My chosen people. These souls who refuse to accept Me will experience a living Hell on earth at the hands of the demons and My chastisements. Come to Me, My children, before it is too late and you fall into Satan's snare."*

I could see some people being marched off for execution at the hands of the evil ones. I then saw them buried in specially marked graves meant to demean them. Jesus said: *"My people, there will be many martyred for My Name's sake. The evil men will taunt you for believing in Me. These evil ones will be confounded as later I will remove your shame by raising up My martyrs in their glorified bodies. Those who were cursed by men will be raised up above the carcasses of the dead unbelievers. Rejoice that you will be given the strength to endure these trials, even if you are asked to die for Me."*

I could see some churches and many had the crosses on top of the steeples torn down. Jesus said: *"My people, My Church will be persecuted as never before. Your churches will be desecrated and changed into museums or burned down. Only a few will be spared that are places of holy ground. When you see this persecution come, you will need to flee the cities to your underground churches. For those who escape martyrdom, I will protect you from harm by the wicked men of your age. You will be in discomfort for a while, but I will lead you to a place of milk and honey beyond your dreams."*

I could see some guns and tanks being used in war. Jesus said: *"My people, many militants will challenge the people seeking peaceful settlements. By their antagonism they will lead you into a planned war by the one world people. There will be chaos then in your nations both for money and food. This will lead to the Antichrist's takeover which is coming soon."*

I could see some beautiful flowers in a field. Jesus said: *"My people, you have enjoyed a long time without any major wars. You will be lulled into the existing peace arrangements. Then there will be sudden destruction, when you least expect it. The evil men are planning a massive takeover when your troops and arms have been stripped from you. Beware an uneasy peace which will turn into a world dictatorship."*

I could see Mary trying to protect her children from the serpent. Mary said: *"My dear children, I will call on my Son's help during the tribulation to protect the little children from the evil one's grasp. He will strike at them, but my foot will crush his head in his attempt. Pray to stop your abortions, for these little martyrs are calling out for my Son's justice. Stop the killing, my children, before my Son's punishments will befall you."*

I could see some kings wearing their crowns and they were all in the dark. Jesus said: *"My people, these are the evil leaders who are in the grasp of the angel of darkness. They have been misled by desires of fame and fortune. God is not in their hearts, no matter what they say on their lips. This is why I read the heart's intentions, since they are not always known publicly. These evil men will meet their just punishments for their wicked deeds. You will not find justice on the earth until My intervention brings everyone to their knees. Only then will the evil ones be cast into Hell by My avenging angels. My faithful will then come into the light of a renewed earth. Pray for this day of joy to come quickly."*

Wednesday, November 26, 1997: (MENES, TECKEL, PERES)
After Communion, I could see a knife in a wall and blood was oozing out of the wall. Jesus said: *"America, you are one of the countries to be divided and fall for your many sins of abortion. You have worshiped the gods of money and pleasure in offering up the blood of your infants. Did you not think that I would bring My justice upon you? Your days are numbered as well, and you will no longer enjoy your freedoms. By your own acts of killing My babies, you have condemned yourselves with this modern day holocaust. What is even more appalling is that many will still ask why My justice is harsh, and they do not recognize all the evil of your killing. Your leaders are such masters of deceit, that these abortions are not even thought of as a great evil that My justice calls for your punishment. There will come a time when all of your riches will be stripped from you, since your god of money will be dashed to failure. Your economic system will be turned upside down and your country turned into a puppet police state. Religious persecution will reign and all of your freedoms will be lost. Your time to pay for your sins is upon you. Pray now for My angels to help you. Prepare spiritually in seeking forgiveness of your sins, so you will be spared My wrath."*

Thursday, November 27, 1997: (Thanksgiving)
After Communion, I could see Jesus carrying a lamb out into the desert. The next scene was a basket of food. Jesus said: *"My people, you have depended on My help for many years. Do you*

*think that I will not help you in these days of tribulation? I tell
you that My help will be even more than you need. If you can
give gracious gifts to your children, how much more will your
Heavenly Father give you all that you need, even if it be in the
wilderness. Give thanks to Me for being at your side throughout
all of your lives. Give all the praise and glory to Me for your
many gifts. Pray even for your trials that you must suffer in the
end days. You may suffer persecution for My Name's sake, but I
will reward you for your faithfulness with more than you could
dream of."*

Later, at Adoration, I could see a door being closed. Jesus said:
*"My people, enter through the narrow gate if you expect to come
to Heaven. It is not easy to follow My ways, because you will be
tested by persecution for believing in Me. Many will criticize you
for this belief in Me, but it is important to remain faithful to all of
My commands. When you are put to the test, be willing to sacrifice everything for Me. It is giving of self and replacing it by My
love that I am drawing you to discover. Many graces are bestowed
upon you for visiting My most Blessed Sacrament. Seek Me where
I can be found and you will discover a trust in Me that will bring
you through life to Heaven. I am always here in My tabernacle
waiting to give you My blessings."*

Friday, November 28, 1997:

After Communion, I could see a sinister man dressed in black.
Jesus said: *"My people, you are seeing the Antipope or false witness displayed before you. He will mislead the people and his
description as the single horn of the Apocalypse fits the readings
of today. Your evil age will increase in its intensity for a short
time. Then My triumph will dash him and the Antichrist's kingdom to pieces. For a while this evil pope will cause a schism in
My Church. He will spew blasphemies from his mouth and he
will be in league with the Antichrist as the desolation of abominations will afflict My Church. He will claim heresies as law and
try to get the people to disobey My laws. For these acts he will be
dashed into Hell along with the Antichrist and Satan. Beware of
the lies and the guile of this pope who will try to destroy even My
remnant. My pope son, John Paul II, will still lead My Remnant*

Church from exile. My faithful will still believe him to be the real pope and My mother will watch over him. Prepare for these end days that will test your faith. It is only by My help that you will keep your faith."

Later, at Adoration, I could see a small truck without back windows as it came to pick up prisoners. Jesus said: *"My children, I have told you before not to be so concerned with dates. Everything will happen when and how I wish it to without any prompting from man. I have told you of the events that will be speeding up. You must have patience for when these events will take place. You have prayed for the tribulation to come sooner, but it will be at your door soon. When your time of persecution arrives, your suffering will seem to lengthen the time of your trial. Some will be martyred as examples to the rest. Some will be tortured, while others will be enslaved. When this trial comes, you will wonder why you desired it sooner, since pain and agony will be all around you. I will give you My comforting words even with the Antichrist at the door. Keep faithful to Me and you will have nothing to fear."*

Saturday, November 29, 1997:

After Communion, I could see the underside of a car where there was the muffler and the gas tank. Jesus said: *"My people, many of you are like this car that I am showing you. When you look at the upper part of a car, all looks sparkling and beautiful, while the underbody is not so pretty. So it is with people. They put on a good front of beauty and how friendly they are. But deep down the heart harbors hate, envy, and jealousies. I am not like your neighbor, whom you can deceive and hide things from. I see into the heart and I know of all of your intentions and all your evil deeds. Do not think that you can do anything without My knowledge. Because I am your judge and also the one who made you and loves you, be on guard at all times to follow My commands and My direction for your life. When you follow My ways out of love and respect, you will have nothing to hide and you will be proud to love everyone and witness as My disciple. Love should permeate through all that you do. When you show love for Me and your neighbor in all that you do, you will not be far from My kingdom."*

Later, at Adoration, I could see an evil eye of a devil as a wolf. Jesus said: *"My people, I wish to warn you about the coming of the Antichrist and his declaration time. At the time of his first announcement about his coming in declaration, have all of your cables out of your house and do not watch your television any longer — disconnect them. As it comes closer to the day of his declaration, do away with your telephone lines, your computers, faxes, copiers, radios, and anything electronic that can be influenced by demons, since they will use them to distract you. In addition to these, stop your paper and even your mail. All of these again will be controlled. Remember, when you see My warning, Pope John Paul II leaving Rome, and the placement of the chips in the hand, you are to pack your sacramentals and your physical needs, ready to go into hiding. Do not have any credit cards, smart cards, nor anyone with a chip in their body, since you can be tracked by these devices. Pray much during this trial for My help and I will instruct your angels where to take you for spiritual safety. This is a time to follow My instructions for helping to save your soul and those of your loved ones and friends."*

Sunday, November 30, 1997: (First Sunday of Advent)
After Communion, I could see a picture of the Infant of Prague dressed as the Infant King. Jesus said: *"My people, I am King of All Nations whether I come as an infant or as a young man. When I was born into your world, My kingdom was present to you. Wherever you find Me, My kingdom is present. My love reaches out to you during this Advent Season in a special and personal way. You love to see babies in your way of cuddling them. This is why I want to love you in a more intimate way. When you prepare for My coming, think of the spiritual gifts that you can present to Me. Your thanks for life and your love are the most treasured gifts that I desire from you. Celebrate this season of love as you prepare to commemorate My coming at Christmas, but also continue your preparation for even My Second Coming. You know not the day of My triumph when I will change over the earth. By your frequent Confessions you can keep your souls replenished with My graces and free from sin. Seek My forgiveness and have contrition for your sins. It is My coming that has re-*

deemed all of you sinners. Come and accept Me at the crib as your true Savior, and Christmas will open a new spiritual dimension in your life."

Later, at Adoration, I saw a bank teller's window and no one was around. Jesus said: *"My people, you rely on your banks and your investments to store your money. In a short time, there will be no safe place for your money. The one world people will contrive a crash of stocks and banks that will cause chaos throughout the world. Many life savings will be stolen by their manipulation. There will be such a panic that the worldly will welcome the Antichrist to bring peace to the turmoil. It is during this upheaval that the Antichrist will take over as a dictator over all the nations in the name of peace. All of this will be planned by the Antichrist's agents to deliver complete control to him. He will then control the jobs, the food, and the money. His reign will be brief, since I will soon come in triumph to destroy his kingdom and replace it with My own. Pray, My people, to endure this trial, since you will need all of your spiritual strength with My help to win your crown."*

Monday, December 1, 1997:

After Communion, I could see in space an image which I could see through from either side. Jesus said: *"My people, be on guard when the Antichrist comes. He will perform great wonders to get the people to believe that he is Me. Know that many of his ploys will only be illusions of lights and mirrors as with lasers and large holograms. His powers are more limited than will appear. These are warnings about his lies and powers that you may keep faith in Me. My coming in power will far overshadow any of the meek attempts of the supposed ruler of peace. In fact, the Antichrist will be nothing more than a tyrant dictator eager for power over the earth. The most damaging influence will be his confusion that he will spread among the souls of the earth. It will take My help and your persistence in faith to save your souls in this time. No matter what anyone tells you falsely, that I am here or there, you will see Me come in glory among the clouds and there will be no illusions. My power will be complete and the evil ones will be chained in Hell when My triumph puts their reign to flight. Never lose faith in Me, for this trial will test everyone's faith.*

Your promise of Heaven will far outweigh any physical comforts that these demons can promise."

Later, at Adoration, I could see a flame of heavenly love being spread over all here present. The Holy Spirit said: *"I am the Spirit of Love, and I come tonight to share with you My abundant graces of the Spirit. You are in the midst of a battle of good and evil. You need to be strengthened by Jesus and Me, so that you can stand up to the evil of your day. Submit yourself to the trial in Our Names that you will be faithful in leading souls to God. This is a most precious time where a battle for souls is being waged by both the side of good and the side of evil. You have this opportunity to bring souls to God; do not fail in your responsibility. At the end of this battle, you are coming to a new era in which I will reign. God the Father has influenced the ages before His Son. Jesus has had His presence in the Host for two thousand years. Now, in this new era, without evil, you will see My Spirit influence all the faithful children, who will grow in perfection on earth, to make them ready for their entry into Heaven. Rejoice, My children, that this new era will soon be upon you. Keep faithful during this test of the tribulation, and you will have a life in the Spirit that will reward all of your spiritual efforts."*

Tuesday, December 2, 1997:

After Communion, I could see some bread in the distance in multiple loaves. Jesus said: *"My people, do not have any fear of the events to take place. Satan and the Antichrist will have their appointed times, but I will not leave you defenseless. This will be a time when you will have to place your full trust in Me. It is I who will lead you by My heavenly angels, where you will be safe from the demons. I am showing you the bread multiplying, because this is what I will provide for you in your need. Do not take the Mark of the Beast or the smart card as means for food. Rely on what I will provide for your food during the tribulation. When you seek Me in Spiritual Communion, My angel will deliver you My heavenly manna. When you take bread with you, again I will multiply it for your survival. People may criticize you for encouraging others to go into hiding, but the alternative is to be martyred or enslaved in the detention centers. When this declaration time* of the Antichrist comes, you will have to flee from the authorities who will be seeking to place the mark in your right hand. As these events come about, you will see My hand in warning you of these events for your own protection."

Later, at Adoration, I could see the seven swords in a gold circle which represents the Sorrowful Mother. Mary said: *"My dear children, I had to suffer many sorrows in my life, so I know how difficult life can be at times. For some, losing their jobs can be very traumatic, when their homes and their children are threatened. Fear not, even in these trials, your spiritual character will be built up on trusting in my Son. You will not be left to suffer alone. Call on my Son and He will help you in the worst of situations. When you are tested, you must pick yourself up and struggle on the best you can do. Never give up, but pray my Rosary for help. Your prayers will be answered in His time, and He will lead you to greener pastures. Have faith in prayer and much good will be accomplished."*

Wednesday, December 3, 1997:

After Communion, I saw some food being eaten and the remainder put away. Jesus said: *"My people, I have told you that a world famine is coming. You, America, have indeed wasted much food and even failed to grow it for money. My justice will hold you responsible for your actions. I have given you many reasons to store food in preparation for this famine. There will be contrived shortages as well, all in the vain of controlling people. I will always see to your best interest in providing for your needs, even if it is necessary to multiply what little food you do have. You have many injustices even today, in that some countries have plenty while others are starving. No matter how much people try to help others less fortunate, there will always be the poor and inequities of food distribution. By saving food now, you may be helping others later who will rely on your wisdom. It is more important though, that you always be spiritually prepared by frequent Confession. As part of your Advent devotions, you need to confess your sins and have your souls pure for My coming at Christmas. This would be your best gift to Me, that is your sorrow for your sins and your resolution to have them forgiven."*

Thursday, December 4, 1997:

After Communion, I could see a spinning water sprinkler with water being sprayed out from a circle. Jesus said: *"My people, this circular flow of water is symbolic of how you will be seeing more storms than usual across your country. Various places will receive more water than their normal average and cause some flooding. Some storms will be even more severe as indicated by the circular flow. These storms have a good chance to effect even some of your food supplies. These storms will be an additional chastisement for your sins, and also a test of your faith in My help. Even though you are tested, I will protect My faithful in many ways. Listen to the readings and prepare your dwelling of faith on Me as a rock. Those who refuse to follow My ways will be like those who build their houses on sand and will meet with disaster as these storms come."*

Later, at the prayer group, I could see a globe of the earth spinning and it stopped while facing Africa. Mary came and said: *"My dear children, you have seen us leave Israel to stay in Egypt to be away from Herod. You will again see evil reborn in Egypt as the Antichrist declares himself. Prepare, my children, for my coming feast day of my Immaculate Conception. This also is special for your country which is dedicated to me in your National Shrine. Continue in your preparations both for my Son's First Coming at Christmas and his Second Coming as well."*

I could see many sacks of grain in a warehouse. Jesus said: *"My people, there will come a time when this food will be scarce and the food will be guarded in a special warehouse. The one world people will dole out rations of food only to those with the Mark of the Beast. They will use food, wars and shortages to control the people in their world takeover."*

I could see some large towers as man was building a new Tower of Babel. Then I saw some golden stairs leading up to Heaven. Jesus said: *"My people, man is still building his towers in the skyscrapers that he builds as monuments to himself. These men who praise their own work will be confounded in their errors. These structures will be knocked down because they were built for man and not Me. Only My faithful will be invited up the stairway to Heaven."*

I could see some long bridges and some of them also were falling in pieces. Jesus said: *"My people, man again has challenged nature with bridges that are vulnerable to the elements. Many of your bridges will be challenged in the coming storms. All of these things are signs to you that you are in the end times. Be persistent in your prayers, so that you do not forget to say them."*

I could see some demons, but then also some beautiful angels. Jesus said: *"My people, you will be challenged in this battle of good and evil. My angels will be with you to protect you from the demons. See that My power will hold the evil ones in check. They will not have free reign on the earth. Man, by his free will, will still be obliged to accept Me or reject Me. This is your life choice, so that those, who choose Satan, will only have themselves to blame for going to Hell. Keep together in your prayer groups for the strength that you can draw on from each other and Me."*

I could see some large trucks carrying prisoners to the detention centers. Jesus said: *"My people, take care that you prepare your things to go into hiding. This evil lot intends harm to all those who will not take the Mark of the Beast. Again, do not take this chip even under pain of death, since you risk the fires of Gehenna to worship the Antichrist. Be ready to flee quickly as the Antichrist declares himself. It is better to save your soul than to seek the food and riches of this world that Satan will tempt you with."*

I could see some leaders going into battle on their chariots. Jesus said: *"My people, many of your leaders are anxious to save face when challenged by military threats. Fame and power leads them before they realize the anguish of death of the innocent participants. Come to your senses, My people, and refuse to fight these battles for the fortunes of the one world people. These are contrived wars to gain their own ambitions. Pray for My peace to come quickly before you destroy each other."*

Friday, December 5, 1997:

After Communion, I could see some small cars as many people were fleeing from the city. Jesus said: *"My people, as the time of the Antichrist comes, I have told you to flee the cities from your persecutors. In this vision there is a portrayal of that flight, since the Antichrist's agents will seek people to place the Mark of the*

Beast in their body. Those who refuse will be outlaws and they will abuse you in the death camps of their detention centers. This time of evil's reign will force you into hiding for your own protection. My angels will guide you to the safe havens of holy ground or to the caves for shelter. Heed My instructions as the time of tribulation draws closer to reality."

Later, at Adoration, I could see a row of faucets and one large sink. No matter how hard the people tried, they could not wash the blood off of their hands. Jesus said: *"My people, the blood on your hands comes from the many abortions committed in your land. These mothers have guilt on their hands and they cannot deny the sinfulness of their actions. Even if many had these sins for-*

given, they will never forget that taking of life from the womb. Outwardly, they may not seem guilty, but inwardly, they are suffering the stress of their guilt. I have told you that even such sins can be forgiven in Confession, but the mother still cannot forgive herself and must live her whole life in that shadow. The taking of life is the most offensive sin to Me. Those who are guilty of such an action, will be responsible for their sin at the judgment. Pray for such mothers that they are not so harsh on themselves. I forgive your sins, but you can try to discourage others from repeating this abomination."

Saturday, December 6, 1997: (St. Nicholas)

After Communion, I could see a Christmas tree set up in a house, but there were no lights. Jesus said: *"My people, I am the Light of the World. Without My light of love and My Incarnation, you would not have your gift of faith today. I am the one who breathes the light of faith into your life. How could you celebrate Christmas without Me? It is My Coming to redeem you that gives you reason to celebrate. So, when you turn on the lights of your Christmas tree, think of Me as the light and Spirit of Christmas. As I bring My gifts of faith, love and salvation, you too, must bring your gift of love for Me. Love requires the faithfulness of the two parties. I have an infinite love for you. Now, you must show Me how much you love Me by your perseverence and your gifts of mercy to your neighbor. Come, celebrate My feast day, but do not come to the feast with empty hands. Love must be a part of your life both for Me and those around you. With an enthusiastic spirit of love in your heart, you will be able to welcome Me into your heart when I come."*

Later, at the Blessed Sacrament Church in Mohawk, N.Y., after Communion, I could see a woman adoring a diamond necklace. Then I saw a shimmering spirit of a soul, and finally a gleaming Host of the Blessed Sacrament. Jesus said: *"My people, it is important every day to realize what is most valuable in your life. The eyes of the world focus on fame, money and valuable things in terms of net worth. You, My faithful, know that your spiritual life in your soul is the most important to guard from sin. Ever since you came into existence in that one cell in your mother's womb, this has been your walk in faith until your dying day. It is My gift of life in your soul that is your life's focus. Even more valuable than your soul is My Real Presence in the Host that I share Myself with you. Your soul is drawn to Me as the goal of your life after death. You seek to be with Me because in Me lies the only true peace that you can experience. It is in receiving Me in My Blessed Sacrament that I can share My graces with you more fully. In the intimate time in your soul, you can be satisfied in My rest. Seek to always be with Me, because I am the fulfillment of your soul's desire. Again, it is important also that you seek to share Me with other souls, and if possible bring souls to Me through conversion. You know the joy of My love in your heart and it is sharing this love with others that you wish them to come to know Me in the same way. So, come enjoy your Master's love at My Eucharistic Banquet."*

Sunday, December 7, 1997:

At Queen of the Apostles, Frankfort, N.Y., after Communion, I could see the skies parting and Jesus on the clouds. Before Him was a young man as St. John the Baptist. Jesus said: *"My people, this scene is the purpose of your preparation, to welcome Me at My Second Coming. When St. John announced My Coming in the desert, this was his second announcement. The first was his greeting Me in the womb of his mother. St. John's life was one of complete giving in preparing the people for the start of My ministry. He was not afraid to witness to Me even when his life was in peril. You, My people, are being prepared again for My Second Coming. Again, I am sending My prophets among you to seek those that want to repent of their sins. My son, you are being sent out as St. John to preach this same message of conversion. As St. John, your life needs to be dedicated to My service entirely. Your time is short and the people need to hear My message of love again. There is an evil age among you and your life may be in jeopardy for speaking out in My name. But I call on you to go forth and continue preaching My Word until you can no longer go. Seek My help every day in your mission and ask the Holy Spirit for the words that you are to speak. By your dedication and the carrying out of My Will, you will win your crown."*

Later, at Deacon Sam and Mary's chapel in Little Falls, NY, I could see much mud and water that were the result of some flooding. Jesus said: *"My people, why are you surprised to see this storm activity in the west, when I told you it would be coming? You will see these and many more, because the people are not heeding My words of warning. My words will be fulfilled to the last detail in My Scriptures. Many have questioned how soon will these events of the end days take place. I will not give you dates, but by the words of today's song, it will be very soon. Concern yourself most with your spiritual preparation in going to Confession. It is your conversion from sin that will save you. This is My calling to you, as My herald in the desert, to make straight the path to the Lord."*

Monday, December 8, 1997: (Immaculate Conception)
After Communion, I saw a bright light and then a picture of a small fetus. Mary said: *"My dear children, I was dressed in the sun of grace even as I was conceived. The Lord granted me this favor for the preparation of His Coming. He gave me free will to choose to be His mother, but I was always one in His Will right from the beginning. Saying my 'yes' to the angel was a fulfill-*

*ment of my commitment to my Son. It was my public announce-
ment that I was His, living in His Divine Will. My Son was joined
to my heart since I was born. I was consecrated to Him for my
whole life. He is the one who enabled me to be blameless in sin.
His perpetual grace kept me focused on Him at all times. I give
thanks and praise to Jesus for all that He has done for me. You
too, my children, should thank Jesus for the sacraments and the
many gifts that He has bestowed upon you. Bring your gift of
love and praise to Him at His crib and live the call to be perfect
with Him in following His Divine Will."*

Later, I could see a young woman and then a path down a dark
round hallway. Mary said: *"My dear children, raise your heads
and arms to praise your Lord for all the good that He does for
you. You are blessed with my Son's gifts and your faith is your
salvation. Treasure your choice to follow Jesus and never let Him
out of your sight. Pray that you will unite your heart with my
Son's heart in a love that will never end. Give your all to Jesus
and follow His Will in all you do. Live your 'yes' to Him every
day to show how much you love Jesus. You will travel down a
dark valley of tears in this life, but look to my Son to light your
way. By following in Jesus' footsteps and letting Him lead you,
you will be led down a path to Heaven. Live in His promise of
eternal life and you will have all that your soul will ever desire."*

Tuesday, December 9, 1997:

After Communion, I could see down through a blue skylight
into some families as they were preparing for Christmas. Jesus said:
*"My people, I am showing you how I look down into your fami-
lies to see if the spirit of Christmas is alive in your house. This is
a joyful season to celebrate My Coming to earth as your Redeemer.
Rejoice, My people, and be filled with the Holy Spirit. This is the
time when your spiritual life should be uplifted. You should be
concentrating more on your prayer life in Advent. When you are
joined with Me in prayer, you have My rest and peace which is
what My feast day is all about. Do not be like a grinch, always
worried about money and your earthly problems. This is a season of joy and you need to share your loving enthusiasm with
everyone, especially in your own households. The angels are sing-*

ing in praise of My Coming. Take time to visit Me as well in My Blessed Sacrament to share your love with Me."

Later, at Adoration, I could see some rich looking furniture as people were very comfortable with their possessions. Jesus said: *"My people, do not grow accustomed to your riches which will be stripped from you. As long as you are fed and have everything that you need, many do not see the need for God in their lives. It is your affluence and easy living that will suffocate your means to protect yourself from evil. As you start to witness more storms, financial hardships, and lost jobs, many will be shocked out of their comfort zone. As events start to accelerate, man will see how vulnerable he is, and he will seek My help. Those used to having the easy life may be drawn to follow the Antichrist, who will promise them lies instead of help. Seek your heavenly treasures and you will never be disappointed in your trials. Never take the Mark of the Beast or follow the Antichrist's lies. He will offer peace and food only through him. Be far away from his influence by fleeing the cities to your refuges. Follow Me only and My angels will protect you."*

Wednesday, December 10, 1997:

After Communion, I could see a trumpet sounding a call both for Christmas and the Second Coming. Jesus said: *"My people, the angels go before you sounding their trumpets of announcement. They herald My Coming at Christmas and they are starting to fulfill their roles in Revelation. As the end days draw upon you, all of the trumpets and scrolls are about to be unleashed. Now is the time to make yourself familiar with these texts, so you can read the signs of the times. Heaven is as anxious as you are to draw down the curtain on evil's allotted time. The angels are rejoicing that My justice will bring this evil reign to an end. My angels will provide you protection, but they will not violate your free will. Rejoice again, My people, for your time of My visitation is near."*

Thursday, December 11, 1997:

After Communion, I could see a stairway and Jesus was coming down to us from Heaven. Jesus said: *"My people, you should be thankful for My Incarnation as a man. I love you so much that I wanted to share in your pain and grief of life. I was willing to even offer My life that all of you would be open to salvation. If you could be changed into a dog, it would show you just a little, how much I had to condescend Myself to be a man. I did not give up My Divinity, but I became a worm of a man for you, so you could know that I suffered as you do. This is empathy to the extreme in sharing your existence with its limitations of the body. I did not have sin as you do from Adam's sin. I am an example of love personified for you to follow. So welcome Me into your hearts as I shared My love with you when I came to Bethlehem. This is the day that God has made, so that all mankind may be able to enter the Gates of Heaven by My Blood."*

At the prayer group, I could see black vultures circling above. Jesus said: *"My people, the birds of prey are circling as the embers for war are enkindled. The world has become tense over many divisions throughout the nations. Many have prepared themselves for war and it will not take much to start a world war. It is important that prayer for peace be among your petitions. My peace will only come when men are more loving toward their neighbor. Seek My peace and not that of the world or the Antichrist."*

I could see Mary as in the image of Guadalupe dressed in the sun. Mary said: *"My dear children, this is an image of when I carried Jesus and I was in waiting for his First Coming. My Son has blessed me with many gifts of His love, which I share with each of you. Be in readiness for His Coming with a proper spiritual preparation in Advent. Also, I am asking you even to be ready for His Second Coming."*

I could see a triangle representing the Trinity and Jesus on the cross was in the middle of the triangle. Jesus said: *"My people, God the Father, Myself, and God the Holy Spirit are always with you because you are linked to Our Being. You are celebrating the joy of My birth coming into the world, but I really was born to die for you. It is My Resurrection that has returned a spiritual light to your darkness of sin."*

I could see a fence placed around a house. Jesus said: *"My people, do not fence yourself in from helping those around you.*

You sometimes have difficulty in accepting others because they may threaten your comfort zone. Be willing to go out of your way to help others without worrying about the constraints of time and money. You only have a short time here to show your love for Me and your neighbor. So do not be selfish, but share yourself with others when you can."

I could see a large globe and it was being nursed as it was sick. Jesus said: *"My people, you have fouled your air and water with many abuses and your leaders are realizing man's effect on the environment. Everything I created has a balance, but you, by your excesses, have polluted what I gave you. Now, the errors that you committed are reaping havoc in your weather. You need to be more responsible for your actions both physically and spiritually. When you are in harmony with My Will, all of your problems will dissipate."*

I could see many news reporters with their equipment attending an important event. Jesus said: *"My people, you will soon see a time when your media will be applauding the Antichrist's coming. He will cause many miracles and illusions. Many will believe through his eyes and they will get taken up with his powers. His coming will be a trumpeted event by the people surrounding him. Do not be surprised when this happens, but be ready to avoid him in all of his deceits and lies. Come, seek My help and I will protect your souls from his influence."*

I could see a factory floor and many workers had sad expressions on their faces, as many were losing their jobs. Jesus said: *"My people, do not be disheartened with the loss of your factory jobs. Many of you have been very affluent with the spoils of your labor. As your standard of living is lowered, you will understand how much your country has been blessed. Because of your sins and the ruthless employers, you will suffer in that your wages will decrease. See a lesson in doing with less is better for your spiritual health. Appreciate My blessings and control your sins or you will bring further disaster among you."*

Friday, December 12, 1997: (Our Lady of Guadalupe)

After Communion, I could see a very beautiful image of Mary as an Indian. Mary said: *"My dear children, I came as an Indian with child to give witness to those people of the evil of offering their children in sacrifice to their pagan gods. These beautiful people witnessed my miracle through God and many were converted. This sign, I have given for the Americas, should be seen again where you mothers are again offering your children up in abortion to your new gods of money, materialism, and selfish convenience. Your shallow respect for life weighs heavily against the nations who allow this holocaust. Wake up, my children, to the blood of these children on your hands. Reach out to prevent these abortions in any way that you can discourage them. Pray constantly for this cause or these sins will draw your people into spiritual and physical ruin. Your nations will fall under the weight of your sins if you forget God and abuse His babies."*

Later, at Adoration, I could see a wooden cross and it was slowly disintegrating. Jesus said: *"My people, many of My lambs are being led astray by the cares of the world. You have become so preoccupied with having to succeed at work, that your job pressures are consuming you. Again, many are not satisfied with a moderate living. They wish to seek more earthly things which ultimately do not make them happy. No matter how many jobs each family has, they are always desirous of a better living. Because of your trauma to gain money, your entertainment has also become a preoccupation to spend your free time to the maximum benefit. In all of your time constraints, is it any wonder that your faith has been falling apart? My people, you need to get off your fast paced living and set up your priorities based on My Will instead of your will. When you give your life over to Me, even your difficulties will be bearable. My burden is much lighter than the demands that you put on yourselves. Seek to do only that which is possible. Stop striving for tasks that you could never attain or even need. It is like the rich man who seeks to make more money and is never satisfied because he desires to have more. But what becomes of all the wealth that is amassed? You could never enjoy spending it all and you cannot take it past the grave, so be content with your lot. Only seek the necessities and leave the rest to Me. By building up your faith, you build up your real treasure in Heaven that will not be lost or corrupted."*

Saturday, December 13, 1997:

After Communion, I could see some cracks and wedges. Jesus said: *"My people, I am showing you how you have Me wedged in your life between all of your worldly cares. I am the one who should come first in your priorities, yet many times you think of Me as an after thought. Your spiritual life is more important than all of your daily world tasks. So place them in the proper perspective, and prioritize your duties so that you are following My Will instead of your own. Many times I knock on your door to let Me into your heart, but are you going to tell Me you have no room for Me? It is only by cleaning out your heart of envy, greed, and selfishness that you will have room for My love. Love of Me and your neighbor should take precedence over any of your other desires. For this will be how you are judged, as to how you showed love in your life. So, always go beyond yourself and do not be so worried about having enough money for yourself only. Life is too short to spend it only on your own ambitions. Give of yourself to others and you will be giving yourself to Me."*

Later, at Adoration, I could see the Host in the monstrance and it was spinning with colors shining out from it. Jesus said: *"My people, these spinning lights are a confirmation for you that the events of the last days are coming close. It also means that the events will happen in rapid succession. So, be on guard, My faithful, that My Coming will conclude these events and bring about My triumph. That is why I stress to you many times not to be fearful, but have hope in My help through this tribulation. It is a glorious time to live in My grace. So, be thankful to sing of My glory with the angels."*

Sunday, December 14, 1997:

After Communion, I could see a triangle against the darkness. Jesus said: *"My people, there is joy on earth because the Second Person of the Blessed Trinity has come to redeem your sins. This is cause for rejoicing even among My angels, since those who were in the darkness of sin can see the light of their salvation in Me. Come and share with Me at My crib the love I pour out on all of humanity. It is enough for you to accept Me as your Savior and everything else will be given you. This grace of My First*

*Coming is your blessing that all men and women should rejoice.
My love in your heart is the desire of every soul, so peace may be
among you. It is My help that you can call on and I will direct
you through all of your difficulties. So, be grateful that your God
has sent you these glad tidings that you celebrate each year. Remember, My salvation for you is greater than any other gift that
you could receive. Those who remain faithful to My love will always be assured of My protection."*

Later, at Adoration, I could see a globe of the earth and some
monkeys. Jesus said: *"My people, look around you at how beautiful everything is in My Creation. As you admire the beauty of the
mountains and landscapes, take a look also at the beauty of every
person that you see. Even if you look down on someone, that
person is important, since they are one of My creatures that I
have endowed with life and a soul. Each person is special and
they each deserve your respect, since I treat each of you equally.
Some may be blessed with different talents and may have different capacities for love. I call on all of you to respect all life in the
same way. Do not take life as something you can discard at your
whim. I have a plan for each life and those who violate My plan
will suffer dearly for their crimes. See that all life fits together as
a concert where each life complements the other. This all fits into
My balance of nature. Man in many ways has upset this harmony in his selfish desires. But soon I will restore full order, so
evil and disharmony will be removed. Rejoice, My faithful, who
are awaiting My day of triumph when My full peace will rest on
the earth."*

Monday, December 15, 1997:

After Communion, I could see the corner of a brick wall leading to another direction. Jesus said: *"My people, in life you reach
some time in your job where there is a dead end for advancement
or you are laid off. You are then faced with a new opportunity to
obtain a better paying job, or you would have no money to survive. You are faced with similar circumstances in your spiritual
life. You have lost your faith in God, or some habit or vice has a
grip on you. You need to change your goals or you will be headed
down a path to Hell. It is at that point in your life that you see*

that I am your only hope. You cannot make it through life on your own. You need My help to lift you up on your feet toward a new path where I will lead you to Heaven. Once you are on the straight and narrow path of My Will, you will see that it is the easiest way to follow. On your old path you stumbled and fell continuously without anyone to help you. On My path, you may falter, but I will lift you up to ease any of your pain. You may suffer on either path, but your reward in Heaven will far out-weigh the eternal suffering in Hell."

Later, at Adoration, I could see an old car in the darkness. Jesus said: *"My people, each year the genealogy of My chosen people is read from David to My blessed Joseph and Mary. It is good to see My roots in the prophecy of the Messiah. Everything had to be fulfilled in Me for that which was foretold. I have passed on a legacy of Faith to you down through the ages as well. See that you keep with these traditions of following My Commandments and take advantage of the sacraments which I instituted for you. Christmas is a time to remember why I came into this world, and it also points to the day of My Second Coming as well. I ask you if I will find any faith in you when I return? Be content with this way of life that I have shown you to love one another. Without love in your life, you are nothing. So seek Me in this Divine Love that I have for you and be ever focused on your Christian heri-tage. Follow Me to Calvary and start with your visit to My crib."*

Tuesday, December 16, 1997:

After Communion, I could see a black seat and then a sinister looking man in a hood in the darkness. Jesus said: *"My people, you are living in an age of apostasy where few are following My commands. This is an evil age that will reach its height with the appearance of the Antipope and the Antichrist. I will allow for a time even for the corruption of a false witness on the throne of My Apostle Peter. Yet, My pope son, John Paul II will continue to lead My Remnant Church, since I will protect My Church to the end. Do not be misled by the imposter pope who will do away with all of the Church's traditional teachings. By his tongue of lies, you will know this evil, black pope as one not to follow, no matter how many will follow him. Take courage, My children, for you will have to defend My teachings as proper in an unpopular environment. You may even be tested with martyrdom to proclaim your belief in My Name. Continue to give worship to Me only and you will save your soul. I will bring all of My faithful through the tribulation to enjoy My era of true spiritual peace."*

Later, at Adoration, I could see several people suffering on crosses. Jesus said: *"My people, you were not placed on this earth only to live an easy life. I have shown you by My suffering and those of the saints that you must struggle and suffer to gain your crown in Heaven. You are to be tried as fire has to purify gold. You are like a rough cut gem which needs to be cut and polished until you are presentable to Me. So, My friends, expect suffering along with the joy of bringing souls to Me. You understand that a soul's life is so important, and it is drawn to Me by natural inclination. But worldly cares and distractions can lead you away from Me. So, always review each day what you are doing for Me. Give yourself time for prayer and then time for your necessities. I need to be at the center of your life, so you never lose focus on why you are here and where you are going."*

Wednesday, December 17, 1997:

After Communion, I could see some traveling bags. Jesus said: *"My people, many of the things that I had to suffer, you will have to suffer also for My Name's sake. Even My birth place was a cause for concern to My parents, since they had to follow the edict of the Romans for registering. You also, will experience harassments in your travel plans as the authorities will become more restrictive in your movements. Then, as I had to flee from Herod to Egypt, you also will have to flee from your homes to escape being killed. The evil leaders of your day do not want to see Christianity spread. So, they will try to discourage your religious expression even to the point of persecution for your beliefs. I have warned you many times that your evil age will be influenced by the Antichrist. Once he declares himself, your lives will be in jeopardy. Seek My help and that of your guardian angels at that time, and I will lead you to safety. Unless you wish to be martyrs, you may have to leave the comfort of your homes and hide in the wilderness. The safe havens and caves await you for your protection. Rejoice at that time, for My triumph will be close at hand to bring you to My Era of Peace."*

Thursday, December 18, 1997:

After Communion, I could see a bright light over the globe of the earth. I could look closer and a beautiful blue glow covered the new era with teeming vegetation. Jesus said: *"My people, you will rejoice to see My day after My triumph and the earth is renewed. I am showing you a glimpse of what this world will look like. You will not know real comfort until you live in My true peace. This world will be a world in harmony with Me where evil and wars will no longer occur. You will marvel in the joy of My love as man will grow in his spirituality according to My Divine Will. This will truly be your preparation to go to Heaven. All of your good intentions to live a better life in the Spirit will be realized in a short time. Have faith and hope in Me and you will share in this paradise. Your life in this new era will focus on Me and no longer will it focus on your artificial materialism. My resurrected saints will lead you in a prayer life of adoration that you could only dream of today. Come, enter into My rest for all those who struggle to know Me in an evil age."*

Thursday, December 18, 1997:

At the prayer group, I could see God the Father in majesty as He blessed the earth with the coming of His Son. God the Father said: *"I Am Who Am comes to you tonight to thank you for remembering Me in your prayer group. Look on this time of year as an inspiration to carry on in the dark of an otherwise dreary winter. This celebration of My Son's Coming is My gift of My Son to all of mankind. Without His Coming and the sacrifice of His Body and Blood, you could not be saved. As you thank Jesus for His coming, thank Me also for sending you My only begotten Son. This fulfillment of the promised Messiah in Jesus was rejected by man. This man of no sin threatened the authority of the chief priests. Even today, My Son's Coming and His way of life is still being rejected by man."*

I could see some huge snow storms on a wooded mountainside. Jesus said: *"My people, you will be tested with some severe storms.*

Your world in its sin, is so unsettled that even your weather reflects your violence and little care for life. If you accept Me at the crib, you must also accept all of the little ones that I send you. When you kill one of these little ones, you are killing a part of My body."

I could see Mary with child being carried on the donkey. Mary said: *"My dear children, I carried my Son to term even though there was an issue of His parentage. I even put up with traveling at a difficult time. When you give everything to Jesus, you do not worry about all of your problems and inconveniences. Bring your babies to term, since you have much better ways to care for children. Do not be selfish with your time or convenience in wanting to kill these little babies. Jesus calls for you to repent and stop this sin as He forgave the woman of adultery. If you can stop your abortions, you will see less chastisements."*

I could see a woman and she was turned completely white as Lot's wife. Jesus said: *"My people, many of your mothers who had abortions are like Eve who listened to the cunning lies of the Serpent. Do not be taken in by the wiles of the Evil One in killing your babies. The Devil tells you that babies in the womb are not human and that having a baby aborted is acceptable in your society. Change your death culture into one of the living. As you see Me come in the crib, your gift to Me could be your allowing all life to live."*

I could see some people in the old days worshiping Greek gods. Jesus said: *"My people, you are no different than the pagans who worshiped idols of long ago. Today, you worship the idols of money, fame, and sports to name a few. Remember, My First Commandment is to worship Me only. If you praise the things of the world more than Me, you are idol worshipers yourselves. Keep Me in focus as your only one God and everything else will be given you."*

I could see some glittering diamonds and precious gems in the stores. Jesus said: *"My people, do not chase after all that glitters in the world. Seek the beauty of heavenly treasures. You want to give rich gifts to your friends who can repay you. Seek to help the poor and less fortunate, and your reward will be stored in Heaven because you will not expect anything in return. These gifts of self are more beautiful than the most expensive gifts that you could buy.*"

I could see a young little girl playing in a sunlit room. Jesus said: "*My people, children are your most blessed gifts that I could send you. Do not abuse My children, but treat them with your most precious care, since I only lend them to you for a short time. See that they are led to Me in the Mass and the sacraments. Treat My gifts with respect and guard them from the Evil One. Bring them up in the Faith and share the legacy of My love with them. Bring them to My crib to adore Me and not just for their Christmas gifts.*"

Friday, December 19, 1997:

After Communion, I could see a dock for boats in the fall. The scene gradually moved out into deeper waters with tall waves. Jesus said: "*My people, when you come to Me, it is like protecting you in a harbor of love. But when your sin takes over, you drift out to sea and are beset by the storms in deep waters. See by the turmoil of your life's decisions that you return to Me in the safety of the shallow water. Do not let the distractions of the world lead you adrift. When trouble comes, you will not be able to handle life's problems on your own. You will be tossed about by the waves where your spiritual life will be in peril. Ask Me, like the Apostles, to calm the waters, which can only happen if you have faith in My help. You know that I control everything. Why do you insist on being away from Me? Admit your failures based on pride and submit yourselves to My Will. Then life will be calm in the arms of My embrace. Come to My love and I will share My abundant graces with you.*"

Later, at Adoration, I could see a man standing at a crossroads deciding which path to take. Jesus said: "*My people, you are buffeted by many decisions every day. With each decision you are either choosing to follow Me or reject Me. Others will try to influence you, even religious people who should know better. You need to test the spirit of whatever advice people give you. How does what they say stand up to the traditions of My Church and My Commandments. If others are teaching you lies or things against My Laws, then disregard their advice and follow My way.*

Do not let others lead you down the wrong path, even if they be some of My clergy. You are the one who has to have an accounting of your actions. You are making the decisions on which you will be judged. Look to Me for help in prayer when you are uncertain which course to take. When you follow My teachings, be not afraid to be different and show people that you are led by love for Me and your neighbor."

Saturday, December 20, 1997:

After Communion, I could see a beautiful glow of light over a crib scene in a cave. This vision of peace lasted a long time and the light did not have any apparent source. Jesus said: *"My people, I am showing you the peace and love I have for all My souls. Come and share My light of My Spirit as you come to this cave at Bethlehem. This is an example to you how I wish to shelter all of My faithful. The angels call out their praise to Me and they are ever ready to do My bidding. When I ask them to lead you to the caves, they will help you in all of your needs. Fear not where you are to go or what you are to say. I will provide your shelter and give you My words so that you will have a golden tongue when you need to confront the evil ones. Have faith in Me and My peace will reign with you."*

Later, at Nocturnal Adoration, I could see a dark gold circling mass and in the middle was Jesus on the cross. Jesus said: *"My people, this circling mass is a sign of the coming warning. I am in the middle of this sign because I suffered for you and now you will see Me in your mini-judgment. Prepare now by going to Confession frequently and build up your spiritual armor with prayer and your sacramentals. Those who have mortal sin on their soul at the time of the warning will have the same experience as the priest who was condemned to Hell. They will see themselves as spiritually dead in a traumatic feeling to see the Hell fire they are destined for, if they do not change their ways. Wake the souls in serious sin, or these souls will experience this deep sense of rejection by God. I am perfection and where I am, people in great sin cannot abide. I am sharing My love with all of you in the mercy of a second chance. But those who refuse Me will have to pay the price in Hell according to My justice. Strive to convert souls at the warning, because this will be the last chance for many evil souls."*

Sunday, December 21, 1997:

After Communion, I could see people kneeling in prayer after Communion. Jesus said: *"My people, after receiving Me in Holy Communion you need to kneel in prayer, so I can be united with you in your heart. Do not be in haste at this time of the Mass. Be reverent and respectful, since My Real Presence is with you at that time. Give time to Me then, so I can communicate with your soul how I wish to lead your life. By not taking this time to heart, how can you listen to My Will for you? Those who do not spend some time with Me are not recognizing the importance of My Real Presence. If you have time, it is even appropriate that you spend some time giving Me thanks in front of My Blessed Sacrament before you leave. Most people are quick to take My gifts and leave, but few remain to give Me thanks for all I have given them. So, My friends, stay close to Me in My Eucharistic Presence for this is the reservoir of all of your graces."*

Later, at Adoration, I could see football players playing a game. Jesus said: *"My people, many of you know of the terms offense and defense both in sports and wars. As the end times approach, you will see a great battle forming between the forces of good and the forces of evil. You can call on Me and My angels to defend your souls from the evil spirits. There will be a great struggle for souls and you need to arm yourselves for this battle. Use your Rosaries, crucifixes, Bibles, and holy water as your weapons. My faithful, have nothing to fear when I am leading you to victory. You know the outcome of the battle will be My triumph and those, who do not follow Me, will scatter in defeat as Satan will be chained. So come, prepare My people, for the great battle is about to begin."*

Monday, December 22, 1997:

After Communion, I saw an old man as relatives gathered for the holidays. I then saw a horn of plenty as many foods were brought out for dinner. Jesus said: *"My people, it is good for you to gather around the table to give thanks as the family is drawn together for the holidays. For some it is a happy event to celebrate, while for others, it is a lonely event. Make an effort to join with each other in celebration of My birthday. This Coming of Mine was an answer to My promise of your redemption. I came to die for you, so rejoice that I have embraced you with My Divine Love. All humanity is joyous at this time, but I hope this spirit of love and friendship would carry out through the whole year. Help those that are alone and needy, especially those in your own family. Let there be true peace and happiness on earth where love needs to be ignited."*

Later, at Adoration, I could see a river come to a falls and it seemed like the souls were coming over the falls into the abyss. Jesus said: *"My people, you are seeing many souls as they fall unsuspectingly into the abyss of Hell. So many souls do not understand about their spiritual lives and how their actions offend Me. You know that if you abuse your body with drinking and drugs, that you may die an early death. When you abuse your spiritual body, it gets sick with sin as well. So, in life you need to keep a healthy body and a healthy spirit body as well. If you keep focused more on Me than your selfish desires, you will find the proper path to Heaven. If you flounder aimlessly in your spiritual life, you will find yourself going over the edge into Hell when you least suspect it."*

Tuesday, December 23, 1997:

After Communion, I could see a crowd gathered for Mass and they looked like sheep without a shepherd. Jesus said: *"My people, many of My souls are seeking Me, but these lambs are not being fed any spirituality. There are many movements, even within My clergy, that have discouraged the people's desire for the sacred. You have become so taken up with the social ministry, that the importance of My Real Presence has been put in a back corner. How can the faithful have respect for My Real Presence if the priests are not faithful to Me and their prayer life? My sheep are wandering without much leadership. This New Age mentality and disobedience to My pope son are leading the way for apostasy even in My Churches. Very few Churches will be faithful to My traditions as time goes on. Is it any wonder that they will even* welcome the Antichrist as a man of peace? Do not be discouraged, My faithful, but do not lose your fervor for My True Presence. If you cannot have valid Masses, you may have to go to underground Masses with holy priests. You may eventually have to pray for Spiritual Communion when My angels will deliver you My Real Presence in the manna. Preserve your faith and never let anyone try to steal you away to an unfaithful sheepfold."

Later, at Adoration, I could see someone at a bar with a big mirror where they could see themselves. Jesus said: "My people, when you look in the mirror, you can see yourself as others see you. It is easy to see imperfections in others where you are quick to criticize. It is much harder to look at yourselves with the same critical eye that you view others with. So, do not be so quick to criticize, for you may be guilty of the same things, and you could be a hypocrite for not practicing what you preach. Be careful not to judge others, because it is My place to make such judgments. You can give some friendly advice, but without malicious intent. Teach others by your own good example, and they may follow what you advise. Recollect yourself each day at night to see how you can improve on your own deeds. Having done so, you will have a much clearer conscience on how to follow Me."

Wednesday, December 24, 1997:

After Communion, I could see a Santa Claus and a Christmas tree. Later, I could see a sign of a crib scene in Bethlehem. Jesus said: "My people, you have many symbols for Christmas and your time is preoccupied with the preparation of gifts. Always remember to display the real sign of Christmas in My crib sign. Teach the children of the real importance of My Coming for man's salvation, rather than just the reception of toys. If you want to truly share Christmas, come to Mass this day, so you can visit Me in person at My Eucharistic Presence. Receive Me into your heart and accept Me as your Savior, and you will have My gift of spiritual life, which is beyond comparison to any other gift. I offer man My gift of eternal life. How could you refuse My graciousness? Repent of your sins, and seek My forgiveness in Confession and you will have all that you ever need in this life. Encourage all souls to come to Me in this way, and Heaven will rejoice at the conversion of even one *soul. Continue, My son, to go out and evangelize the people as St. John the Baptist, and your joy will be complete as well."*

Later, at Midnight Mass, after Communion, I could see some tents as the Covenant and a stream of muddy rain water. Jesus said: *"My people, you are seeing the Ark of the Covenant in this vision of My tents of the Holy of Holies. I have promised man that a redeemer would be sent to free you of your sins, since the time of Adams's first Original Sin. My birth on earth was the fulfillment of that promise. I am the Messiah foretold in the Scriptures, that would visit My people and bring them the chance for eternal life. Do not refuse Me when I knock on the door of your heart and soul, but open your mind to accept Me. The stream is an example of how much you are tested by the Evil One. If you are not well-grounded in faith in Me, how can you stand up to the intentions of the Evil One to destroy you? Build your faith on the rock of faith in Me, and do not be swept away by unbelief or the lies of the Evil One."*

Thursday, December 25, 1997: (Christmas Day)

After Communion, I could see a peaceful night and in the sky I could see a red sanctuary light burning. Jesus said: *"My people, My Presence is among you at My crib in Bethlehem. That is the significance of the burning red sanctuary light. I am the Light of the World and your promise of salvation through Me. Receive Me in Holy Communion and again you will experience My Real Presence at the crib. I am present in all the tabernacles of the world, and I will continue to be present to you even to the end of time. Give thanks and praise for My Real Presence, for this is how I am with you at all times. Never doubt that I am always standing near your side, ever ready to help you in your need. Just call on Me, and by your invitation I will see to answer your prayer in My time and what is best for your soul. Rejoice, My people, for the blessing of My Presence is among you."*

Later, at Adoration, I could see a big large pit and some machinery with a blue light. It kept falling deeper into the pit and disappeared. Jesus said: *"My people, you are seeing how your technology will lead you into a financial meltdown. Just as you have seen a meltdown in a nuclear plant, you will also see how all of your advances will fall in on itself. This is because man today, has built a structure of machines to answer all of his needs. The main problem is that this structure was not of My making, nor am I a part of many people's lives. That is why this life of money and technology will fail, because it is godless. You already are seeing the signs of this destruction in the failures of those greedy to make money at any cost, even at the expense of their souls. I have told you many times, what does it profit a man to gain the whole world and lose his soul in the process? Pray, My people, for when this destruction comes, the Antichrist will use this opportunity to gain control by his leadership."*

Friday, December 26, 1997: (St. Stephen)

After Communion, I could see an angel in all of its splendor. I asked Jesus' permission for my angel, Mark, to speak. Mark said: *"I stand before God and share your joy and praise of Jesus on the commemoration of His birth. I am here for your protection, especially in any times of persecution. You know as the time of the Antichrist draws near, that many will cause you troubles where you intend to speak. But continue on in your dedication to evangelize souls for Jesus. Be not afraid of these evil men, but rely on the Holy Spirit and Myself for your speech and perseverence even in your moment of testing. Have faith and trust in Jesus' help that many will be converted in this last hour for souls. Let your example of faith lead others to Jesus. Never let up in your work, for there is not much longer for you to save souls."*

Later, at Adoration, I could see a vision of strange lights that were magenta colored. There were strange signs of the illusions of the Antichrist. Jesus said: *"My people, do not be taken in by the man who will claim that he is the Christ. This Antichrist will come with many tricks and illusions to mislead the people into following him. He will be the head of the New Age Movement and try to force his one world religion on everyone. Do not watch him on TV, listen to him on the radio, or read his literature. He will have superhuman powers of persuasion. That is why you need to stay away from his influence. Seek out My help and My power, and I will protect your souls. The Antichrist's power will be fleeting, as I will bring him to submission. Bear with this test but a short time and My victory will soon usher in an Era of*

Peace. Seek the Divine Love and power which will overtake any earthly or evil power that will be dashed to Hell in chains. Stay close to My side and you will gain the spoils of My victory. Those who worship money and the evil one will only enjoy pleasure for a moment. The price of that moment will be eternal lose of their soul in Hell. Any earthly riches will go up in smoke and never yield anything of lasting value. Instead, invest your time and good works in My behalf and you will reap heavenly treasures beyond anything of earth. So do not let money distract your work on earth. Be content with your lot and you will seek the better portion following My Will instead of your own."

Saturday, December 27, 1997: (St. John the Apostle)
After Communion, I could see Our Lady's face up close. Mary said: *"My dear children, St. John was given to help me in my later years. He is a strong model of hope and faith in my Son, Jesus. He was sincere in all that he did for my Son and served Him in all of his requests. His writings were very close to the heart of my Son, and he conveyed that special love of Jesus in all that he did. Follow in his footsteps in sharing the word of God in the Gospels. Glory in my Lord and Savior, Jesus, and be always willing to do His Will. All of the saints found their salvation by following the Divine Will. So, they are an example to you that you follow the Divine Will as well. This is the ultimate giving of self that is asked of each soul."*

Later, at Adoration, I could see an old church with statues and stained glass windows. Jesus said: *"My people, see that you keep to My traditional Church in the use of the sacraments and keeping My Commandments. Do not be taken up with modernism or the schismatic church. Many are making man's laws into their own dogmas. All of the new changes being proposed are not necessary. Changing of the Mass in some aspects of the Consecration can even cause an invalid Mass. Stay with the precepts taught by the Apostles and that will be enough to save your soul. When you follow My Will, you are searching for the truth. If you follow the Antipope or the Antichrist, you will be led down a path to Hell. Worship Me only and discard all of your other worldly distractions."*

Sunday, December 28, 1997: (Holy Family Sunday)

After Communion, I could see a ladder and a church burning with the smoke pouring out. Jesus said: *"My people, as you come together at My Eucharist, see how much discord is present even among My churches. You have divisions between different religions and even opposing views within each church. How can you have peace in your faith families, if you still cannot have peace in your individual families? Hatred for people is even being expressed in the burning of churches. For some, these isolated instances are not showing concern, but soon you will realize that this is an organized scheme by the one world people to root out all public religious gatherings. Soon, you will witness religious persecution as you have never seen before. Since many have fallen away or are lax in their faith, an apathy will come over the people where they will not fight for their religious freedoms. Governments will outlaw such religious expression and many will accept these edicts and religion will only be expressed underground. Pray, My people, for strength in this trial. Your gift of faith is too precious to discard, for without love of God and neighbor, your society will crumble under the Antichrist's reign."*

Later, at Adoration, I could see a tractor on a farm. In the streets I could see some protesters. Jesus said: *"My people, many of your small farmers are being crowded out of their markets by cheap prices and expenses that are increasing. These were the same men protesting their plight in losing their farms to bankruptcy. As your food comes under increasing control by only a few rich hands, you will be at the mercy of the one world people for supply and purchase. Food will be used to control people through the chips in buying and selling. Do not fear, My children, I will provide your food through My manna and multiplication of what you have. Do not give in to the Antichrist's Mark of the Beast for food. You will be tested, but those who keep faith in Me will be saved."*

Monday, December 29, 1997:

After Communion, I could see many bells in clusters ringing together. Jesus said: *"My people, the bells of freedom are ringing out the joy of My Coming to free all of mankind from their sins. The Lamb of God came down to earth to be sacrificed, so that you may be saved. All Heaven and earth are rejoicing because the Gates of Heaven are open again to receive the faithful. Now that this grace is yours, it is your free will to choose to accept Me as your Savior and Redeemer. By My blood I have set you free. Do not put aside My saving grace, but accept it into your heart, the love I pour out on each of your souls. Christmas is the joy of My First Coming, but it is a call for you to accept Me and prepare for My Second Coming. You know not the time of My coming judgment, but prepare your souls by seeking My forgiveness of your sins in Confession. Those that pray and follow My Commands are as the good servants who will be welcomed into the banquet of My table in Heaven. Come, share at My table the joy of all of My faithful servants.*"

Later, at Adoration, I could see some race cars. Jesus said: *"My people, all souls are in a race against time and the finish line is your death. You are all appointed a given length of time on earth during which you have to choose between Me or the world. Those who are faithful in prayer and deed can truly say that they have fought the good race and have won their crown in Heaven. When you are trying to save souls, you are in a race with the Devil and time to bring them to Me. Do not give up on any soul until their death, for there is always hope for them to change. But do not wait until it is too late for them to be saved. Better to come to Me now, than expect to be saved later. Now is the acceptable time. You may not have tomorrow to repent.*"

Tuesday, December 30, 1997:

After Communion, I could see Jesus in some golden outlines and then a triple scene representing a person's lifetime. Jesus said: *"My people, you experience life day by day and second by second, but I view your life in its entirety with all of your desires and intentions. When you come to church to visit Me, keep your focus on loving Me and not just to go through the motions. Put your heart into the Mass and every prayer, and I will know you really mean to love Me. Unless you truly love Me and know Me personally, how can I admit you into Heaven, for I will say I do not know you? So keep your focus on My love every day. Live your life consistently loving Me, for I am a daily part of your life if you let Me in to be a part of it. Many souls acknowledge My exist-ence, but few try to show their love for Me. Every soul that re-joices in their heart with My love, causes rejoicing in Heaven for your love of God. See that this Christmas season is a time of ten-der love for Me as the Infant in the crib. Think of Me in this same feeling every day of the year. Your life should be an expression of your love for Me at all times, not just on Sundays at Mass."*

At the prayer group, I could see some toy cars with radio oper-ated devices. Jesus said: *"My people, you parents buy only the best toys for your children at Christmas. Your best gifts to them would be a Rosary and a Bible to help save their souls. You need to train your children more in the ways of Heaven than the ways of the world. Pass on the traditions of the Faith to them and they will have a holy inheritance."*

I could see a new calendar and it was covered with darkness. Jesus said: *"My people, I have told you not to worry about dates, but you will be seeing an increase in evil events in the coming year. Everything happens in My time only and it is directed by the Father. You will need to be spiritually strong as the end days draw closer. Take more time for your private prayer, so you will grow closer in My trust. See that I will guard you and guide you to follow My Will."*

I could see a mother and child with a light shining down on them. Jesus said: *"My people, look at the precious little ones among you and protect them from abuse and from being killed even be-fore they are born. Your country's abortions are a major blemish on all of your blessings. I give you the miracle of new life, but you have been snuffing life out at your convenience. Change your ways, America, or you will live to regret your actions and inac-tion to stop abortions."*

I could see Our Lady and she showed me a bombed out car and then some homes destroyed by tornadoes. Mary said: *"My dear children, you see evil in many killings and then people's homes destroyed by nature. Why is there so much violence in your soci-ety? Look to your TV programming and your movies and what is glorified there but the same violence? These killings displayed by your producers and directors are placing these thoughts and im-ages in the minds of young and older people. By promoting such*

*wicked movies, you are causing the violence around you. You
need to witness to love and peace in order to stop your wars and
killings. Live the Gospel and love will be spread in your world."*

I could see some people who were dejected and frustrated by a
circle of poverty. Jesus said: *"My people, do not forget about the
poor and those less fortunate than yourselves. When you have
time and money, reach out to help them in the agony of their help-
lessness. Many are seeking direction spiritually as well. The spiritually poor also need your help and prayers. Look beyond your
comfort zone to help others in both physical and spiritual need."*

I could see some whitened sepulchers as burial places of the
rich and famous. Jesus said: *"My people, have mercy and pray for
those sinners leading a life of the spiritually dead. Unless you
cast aside your worldly riches, you will not be able to see clearly
how to lead a holy life. It is more difficult for the rich to come to
Me, since they feel that they have all they will ever need. Having
such amounts of money does not insure happiness or lead you to
Heaven. You need to be rich in grace to come to Heaven. Help
those blinded by money to see their false security and alert them
to the forgiveness of sins. Unless the rich change their earthly
goals to heavenly goals, they will remain spiritually dead."*

I could see stars and symbols of astrology and the New Age
Movement. Jesus said: *"My people, as the evil of your age in-
creases, be watchful not to be taken up with strange signs and
crystals. Foretelling the future and reliance on the stars are not
going to lead you to Me. Discard any attempts by those trying to
allure you into the New Age Movement. All of these earthly gods
are idol worship contrary to worshiping Me only. Do not be at-
tracted to their enticing music or their oriental words. These are
the sirens of the evil ones who will lead you only to pagan gods.
Strive to pray and hold fast to your faith and trust in Me. Discard
all of the New Age trinkets and literature."*

Wednesday, December 31, 1997: (New Year's Eve)

After Communion, I could see the face of a man praying as he
was looking up to Heaven. Jesus said: *"My people, you need to
direct your lives to Me in all that you do. Pray every day and give
thanks for both your creation and My saving act of redemption.*

As you begin a new year, look back on the last year to see if you have made any spiritual progress. Measure your success by whether you have grown closer to your Lord, or did you fall further away. Measure, also, your evangelization efforts by how many souls you returned to Me. After recollecting your status, now you know from where to start and I will show you how to improve. How much of your day do you let Me come into your life through prayer? This is where your strength lies, so give yourself time for speaking to Me every day. Only set goals that you feel you are committed enough to keep. You may make more progress in smaller attainable goals than be frustrated in large ideas that you cannot accomplish. Each year set out to root out one vice at a time and your steady progress will bring you to Heaven's Gate."

Later, at Adoration, I could see the pope in a wheel chair. Jesus said: *"My people, My pope son, John Paul II, will deteriorate in his health as evil men will try to remove him. His health is affected by the influence of those around him. This will be used as an excuse to take over his office. There will come in time an evil pope, elected to take Pope John Paul's position. This will be one of the main signs to go into hiding, when this comes about. Even though My Pope son will be exiled, he will still lead my Remnant Church. This new schismatic church, led by the Antipope, will mislead many souls. Stay true to My commands and I will protect the souls of My faithful. Drastic changes in My Church will force My faithful into an underground Church from persecution. Do not lose hope, My children, for just as the Antipope and the Antichrist gain power, I will smite all of these evil doers. Have patience, and you will soon experience My true peace in the Era of Peace that I have promised you."*

Index

Combined Index of Volumes I - IX
Entries with just numbers refer to page numbers in Volume I
all other entries indicate the volume in Roman numerals
along with the date of the entry

Prepare for the Great Tribulation and the Era of Peace

Prepare for the Great Tribulation and the Era of Peace

Prepare for the Great Tribulation and the Era of Peace

Prepare for the Great Tribulation and the Era of Peace

harvest
  protection (St. Michael) — III: 8/13/95
  farmers move to new land (Jesus) — V: 10/24/96
harvest of souls
  prepare for purification (Jesus) — V: 10/3/96
harvesting souls
  convert to dying day (Jesus) — V: 10/20/96
haste — 58
healing — 174
  faith (Holy Spirit) — II: 11/12/94
  gifts (Holy Spirit) — II: 6/4/95
  end time miracles (Jesus) — III: 4/17/96
  physical & spiritual (Jesus) — III: 10/30/95
  in body and spirit (Jesus) — VI: 2/26/97
  use gifts or loose them (Mary) — VI: 2/11/97
  spiritual and physical (Holy Spirit) — IX: 10/28/97
healing ministry
  evangelize all (Jesus) — VI: 3/6/97
healing power
  if not used, will dry up (Jesus) — VII: 4/21/97
healings
  in Jesus' name (Jesus) — III: 5/8/96
  spiritual and physical (Jesus) — III: 6/5/96
  suffering servants/cures (Jesus) — III: 5/22/96
  must heal souls first (Jesus) — IV: 7/31/96
  miraculously answered (Jesus) — V: 12/1/96
  spiritual first/God's Will (Jesus) — V: 10/8/96
  call on His Name (Jesus) — VII: 5/20/97
health
  stress,food,technology (Jesus) — VI: 1/13/97
heart — 97, 136
  attention (Jesus) — II: 9/25/94
  corrupt and pure (Jesus) — III: 2/29/96
  Divine Will,trust,faith (Jesus) — III: 3/11/96
heart recessed
  empty heart (Jesus) — II: 3/4/95
heart
  outside covers up evil (Jesus) — IX: 11/29/97
hearts — 24, 29, 127, 139, 154, 209
  weather (Jesus) — III: 7/27/95
  open to mercy & love (Jesus) — IV: 7/24/96
  ice cold, melt with love (Jesus) — V: 11/8/96

hearts of stone
  love of God decides fate (Jesus) — VII: 6/6/97
hearts opened
  spiritual spring cleaning (Jesus) — VIII: 8/5/97
Heaven — 3, 13, 69, 99, 134, 146, 169, 179, 188, 201, 205, 212
  earth (Jesus) — II: 5/27/95
  Prodigal Son (Jesus) — II: 7/20/94
  beatific vision (Jesus) — III: 5/5/96
  evangelization (Jesus) — III: 2/4/96
  His Key (Jesus) — III: 4/17/96
  little child (Jesus) — III: 1/11/96
  nature (Mary) — III: 8/15/95
  salvation (Jesus) — III: 8/12/95
  the road is bumpy, suffer (Jesus) — VII: 5/23/97
heaven on earth — 21, 95, 108, 199
  Garden of Eden (Jesus) — II: 5/14/95
  beauty and peace (Jesus) — III: 3/20/96
  peace,love,harmony (Jesus) — III: 6/12/96
  angels & safe havens (Jesus) — IV: 9/13/96
heavenly encounter — 221
helicopters
  investigating people (Jesus) — V: 11/14/96
  mapping targets (Jesus) — VIII: 7/26/97
helicopters & satellites
  means of searching (Jesus) — V: 10/29/96
Hell — 15, 22, 54, 55, 87, 144, 212
  rich man (Jesus) — II: 3/16/95
  whirlpool (Jesus) — II: 8/29/94
  evil destroyed (Jesus) — VII: 5/11/97
  path full of good intentions (Jesus) — VIII: 7/25/97
  repent of laziness (Jesus) — VIII: 9/24/97
  understanding eternity (Jesus) — VIII: 7/21/97
  best protection (Jesus) — VIII: 9/1/97
  fall unsuspectingly (Jesus) — IX: 12/22/97
  for those who refuse God (Jesus) — IX: 12/20/97
herald
  remnant (Mary) — II: 7/10/94
  second coming (Mary) — II: 12/23/94
heresies
  speak out against (Jesus) — VI: 1/2/97

118

Prepare for the Great Tribulation and the Era of Peace

Prepare for the Great Tribulation and the Era of Peace

public harassment (Jesus)	III: 8/29/95	police state	
spiritual weapons (Jesus)	III: 10/15/95	UN troops (Jesus)	VII: 5/10/97
personal mission		political leaders	
consolation (St. Therese)	III: 1/18/96	pray for them, corruption (Jesus)	VII: 5/22/97
Peter's denial		pollution	
Baptism of the HolySpirit (Jesus)	III: 1/8/96	nature (Jesus)	III: 10/13/95
physical body		pool of water	
mirror of faults (Jesus)	III: 4/22/96	living water (Jesus)	II: 1/10/95
Pieta		poor	9, 41, 47, 51, 65
humble lamb (Mary)	II: 3/13/95	help food,time,money (Jesus)	III: 3/27/96
Pilgrim Statue of Fatima		relic (St. Eliz Seton)	III: 1/4/96
thanks to workers (Mary)	VIII: 8/28/97	rich (Jesus)	III: 9/22/95
pilgrimage		poor people	
repentance (Jesus)	II: 7/7/94	help them (Jesus)	III: 6/19/96
pilgrimages	106	money & suffering (Jesus)	IV: 8/25/96
pilgrims	123, 140	help in any way, shrine (Mother Cabrini)	V: 11/13/96
pillar of flame		pray and help (Jesus)	VI: 1/31/97
purification (Mary)	II: 7/10/94	share and help (Jesus)	VI: 1/21/97
pine tree		cannot repay you (Jesus)	IX: 12/18/97
praying hands (Jesus)	II: 2/2/95	poor souls	163
pink lightning		Pope	4, 15, 25, 32, 42, 52, 61, 84, 213
Antichrist (Jesus)	II: 11/1/94	John Paul II (Jesus)	II: 11/17/94
place		15 decade rosary (Mary)	III: 10/4/95
pray for leaders (Jesus)	VIII: 8/28/97	Church (Jesus)	III: 9/13/95
plagues		exiled (Jesus)	III: 5/18/96
new era (Jesus)	III: 1/13/96	salvation (Jesus)	III: 10/5/95
snakes and purification (Jesus)	III: 2/3/96	Pope evangelizes	
biological weapons (Jesus)	IX: 11/13/97	vocations (Jesus)	III: 1/5/96
in tribulation (Jesus)	IX: 10/27/97	pope exiled	
of Revelation (Jesus)	IX: 11/5/97	remnant forced out (Jesus)	VII: 6/7/97
unfaithful to suffer most (Jesus)	IX: 11/25/97	Pope John Paul II	
plane crash		deeply tested (Jesus)	II: 11/22/94
worry (Jesus)	II: 7/31/94	apostasy (Jesus)	III: 3/6/96
a witness in prayer (Jesus)	IV: 7/24/96	last pope (Jesus)	IV: 9/17/96
planes	1	schism, exiled from Rome (Jesus)	IV: 8/16/96
planet rings		removed from papacy (Jesus)	V: 10/15/96
resurrection (Jesus)	II: 8/27/94	exile and schism (Jesus)	VI: 2/22/97
planned accidents		follow his teachings (Jesus)	VI: 3/7/97
avoid acts of killing (Jesus)	VII: 6/5/97	follow in faith & morals (Jesus)	VI: 1/2/97
polarization of good & evil		lead remnant Church (Jesus)	VI: 3/20/97
Armageddon (Jesus)	II: 1/24/95	lead, in hiding (Jesus)	VI: 1/4/97
		leads remnant,exiled (Jesus)	VI: 3/22/97

More Messages from God through John Leary

If you would like to take advantage of more precious words from Jesus and Mary and apply them to your lives, read the first three volumes of messages and visions given to us through John's special gift. Each book contains a full year of daily messages and visions. As Jesus and Mary said in volume IV:

Listen to My words of warning, and you will be ready to share in the beauty of the Second Coming. Jesus 7/4/96

I will work miracles of conversion on those who read these books with an open mind. Jesus 9/5/96

Prepare for the Great Tribulation and the Era of Peace

Volume I - *Messages received from July 1993 to June 1994*
ISBN# 1-882972-69-4 . . . . 256pp. - $7.95

Volume II - *Messages received from July 1994 to June 1995*
ISBN# 1-882972-72-4 . . . . 352pp. - $8.95

Volume III - *Messages received from July 1995 to July 10, 1996*
ISBN# 1-882972-77-5 . . . . 384pp. - $8.95

Volume IV - *Messages received from July 11, 1996 to Sept. 30, 1996*
ISBN# 1-882972-91-0 . . . . 104pp. - $2.95

Volume V - *Messages received from Oct. 1, 1996 to Dec. 31, 1996*
ISBN# 1-882972-97-X . . . . 120pp. - $2.95

Volume VI - *Messages received from Jan. 1, 1997 to Mar. 31, 1997*
ISBN# 1-57918-002-7 . . . . 112pp. - $2.95

Volume VII - *Messages received from April 1, 1997 to June 30, 1997*
ISBN# 1-57918-010-8 . . . . 112pp. - $2.95

Volume VIII - *Messages received from July 1, 1997 to September 30, 1997*
ISBN# 1-57918-053-1 . . . . 128pp. - $3.95

Other Great Titles From
QUEENSHIP PUBLISHING
From your local Catholic bookstore or direct from the Publisher

Trial, Tribulation and Triumph
Before, During and After Antichrist
Desmond Birch
ISBN# 1-882972-73-2 .... $19.50

The Amazing Secret of the Souls in Purgatory
An Interview with Maria Simma
Sr. Emmanuel of Medjugorje
ISBN# 1-57918-004-3 .... $4.95

After the Darkness
*A Catholic Novel on the Coming of the Antichrist
and the End of the World*
Rev. Joseph M. Esper
ISBN# 1-57918-048-5 .... $14.95

Mary's Three Gifts to Her Beloved Priests
A Deeper Understanding of Our Lady's Messages to Fr. Gobbi
Rev. Albert Shamon
ISBN# 1-57918-005-1 .... $2.95

The Final Warning
And a Defense Against Modernism
Paul A. Mihalik, Sr., Lt. Colonel USAF (Ret.)
ISBN# 1-57918-043-4 .... $4.95

A Light Shone in the Darkness
*The Story of the Stigmatist and Mystic
Therese Neumann of Konnersreuth*
Doreen Mary Rossman
ISBN# 1-57918-044-2 .... $12.95

A Little Catechism on the Holy Rosary
Miguel Guadalupe
ISBN# 1-882972-78-3 .... $4.95

Call of the Ages
*The Apparitions and Revelations of the Virgin Mary
Foretell the Coming of Evil and an Era of Peace*
Thomas W. Petrisko
ISBN# 1-882972-59-7 .... $11.95